NORTH
AMERICAN
BIRDS

NORTH AMERICAN BIRDS

Patrick Hook

CHARTWELL
BOOKS, INC.

This edition published by:

CHARTWELL BOOKS, INC.
A Division of
BOOK SALES, INC.
276 Fifth Avenue Suite 206
New York, New York 10001

Reprinted 2011

ISBN-13: 978-0-7858-2786-3

© 2007 by Compendium Publishing Ltd.,
43 Frith Street, London W1D 4SA,
United Kingdom

Cataloging-in-Publication data is available from the Library of Congress

Designer: Danny Gillespie
Illustrations: Mark Franklin
Color reproduction: Northern Lights Studio
Printed in: China

PHOTO CREDITS

Getty Images 12, 28, 103, 252; Photographer's Choice: 1, 16, 60, 61, 76, 102, 105, 112, 113, 128, 216, 222, 226, 230, 255; National Geographic: 4, 8, 19, 31, 32, 33, 34, 37, 47, 51, 53, 68, 72, 73, 80, 98, 100, 169, 170(R), 171, 185, 205, 221, 227, 252, 254, 256; Panoramic Images: 6, 14, 172, 190, 192; Discovery Channel Images: 11, 77, 81, 97, 244; Digital Vision: 13, 58, 181; Visuals Unlimited: 26; Aurora: 38, 74; MedioImages: 42, 175, 182, 183, 219; The Image Bank: 44, 54, 70, 107, 110, 129, 130, 174, 220, 225, 231; Photodisc Red: 46, 79, 96, 179, 246; Lonely Planet Images: 64, 170(L), 229; Stone: 67, 177; Altrendo: 69, 212; Robert Harding World Imagery: 75, 78, 218, 223; Science Faction: 94; America 24-7: 101; Photonica: 176; Stockbyte Silver: 180; Visuals Unlimited: 228; Purestock: 245

Corbis Images 45, 50, 52, 63, 89, 91, 92, 114, 115, 125, 126, 155, 157, 162, 163, 164, 166, 167, 178, 188, 206, 207, 208, 241, 250(L); Arthur Morris: 10, 18, 29, 30, 35, 36, 39, 40, 41, 43, 49, 55, 57, 62, 82, 83, 84, 85, 87, 88, 106, 108, 123, 142, 143, 144, 146, 148, 149, 151, 152, 153, 154, 156, 165, 168, 184, 186, 187, 189, 196, 198, 199, 200, 201, 202, 203, 204, 210, 211, 213, 214, 215, 224, 232, 233, 234, 236, 237, 238, 239, 240, 242, 243(L); Gary W. Carter: 21, 22, 145, 158, 159, 160, 161, 243(R); Ron Sanford: 24, 25, 150, 247; Joe McDonald: 27, 56, 131, 133, 136, 137, 138, 141, 250(R); Bob Krist: 48, 195; Visuals Unlimited: 65; Daniel J. Cox: 66, 86; Ralph A. Clevenger: 90; W. Perry Conway: 93; Karen Kasmauski: 104; Steve Kaufman: 109; Richard Hamilton Smith: 116; Roger Tidman: 117, 118; Darrell Gulin: 119, 235; D. Robert & Lorri Franz: 120; Hal Beral: 121(B), 124, 209; Raymond Gehman: 121(T); Frans Lanting: 122; David A. Northcott: 132; Wayne Bennett: 134; Tom Brakefield: 135; George D. Lepp: 139, 140; Carl & Ann Purcell: 194(L&R); Chase Swift: 248; Markus Botzek/zefa: 249; Kennan Ward: 251

GLOSSARY

Bill / Beak
The bill, or beak, forms the outer parts of a bird's mouth, and its shape usually indicates the type of diet it has. Hummingbirds, for instance, have a long, narrow bill suitable for a long tongue, whereas an eagle has a bill that is better suited to ripping meat apart.

Breast
The breast is analogous to the human chest—it houses the main flight muscles. These are attached to the skeletal breastplate, a structure that is only found in birds.

Cap
The cap is the upper part of the head, and since it is often marked with distinctively colored feathers, can be a very useful identification aid.

Collar
The collar is the upper part of the neck, just below the head.

Comb
The comb is a colored area above the eye, and is only found in male birds. Since strong colors can indicate good health, females often use the comb as part of their mate selection process.

Crest
The crest is a tuft of feathers found on a bird's head. The males of some species have very ornate crest structures, and because large tufts can indicate good health, they are often used by females as part of the mate selection process.

Crown
The crown is the top of a bird's head, and can often have vivid coloration.

Flank
The flank is the area along the side of a bird's body, running from the middle to the rear.

Flight feathers
The flight feathers are found on the wings, and are divided into two distinct types—primary and secondary feathers.

Mantle
The mantle is an area on the top of a bird's body that is covered with relatively short feathers. It runs across the back and onto the wings.

Pelagic
Pelagic birds are those species that spend most of their lives over the open ocean. Examples include the albatross, fulmar, jaeger, skua, petrel, and shearwater.

Plumes
The plume feathers found in the males of some species can be very ornate structures. Although their high visibility makes their owners more vulnerable to predators, these decorative features are attractive to females, and so are often used as part of the mate selection process.

Primaries
Primary feathers are found at the end of the wing and play a vital role in helping the bird to fly.

Secondaries
Secondary feathers are found toward the middle of the wing and help generate lift and also contribute toward flight stability.

Tail
A bird's tail is usually made up of long feathers that project rearwards. Some species use these as flying aids, whereas others, such as the peacock, use them for purely decorative purposes.

PAGE 1: A male Red Cardinal perches in the winter snow.

PAGES 2–3: Mankind has been captivated by the flight of birds since time immemorial.

RIGHT: The Bald Eagle is America's national bird—the name derives from the fact that the word "bald" used to mean "white," referring to its head. They are very large birds, with a wingspan of around 80 inches. They are distributed across most of North America, from Alaska and Canada in the north to northern Mexico in the south.

CONTENTS

INTRODUCTION

Introduction

Birds originally evolved from the dinosaurs; however, during this process they developed a number of special adaptations, including lightweight bones, strong breathing mechanisms, powerful flight muscles, and aerodynamically efficient feathers. Birds are warm-blooded, and reproduce by laying eggs. Most build nests and raise their young with great care; however, some such as the cuckoo deposit their eggs in the nests of other species. Until the nestlings have fledged, they are entirely dependent on the parent birds. Some are left to fend for themselves soon after leaving the nest—others stay with their parents for extended periods of time.

In prehistoric times, there were several species of birds that were enormous by modern-day standards. Today the largest are the ostriches—natives of Africa—and the smallest are the hummingbirds. The largest birds found in North America are the cranes and herons, along with the California Condor and the Bald Eagle. There are few places where birds of one kind or another do not thrive. Some—such as the pigeon, do well in the middle of large cities. Others spend almost their entire lives far out at sea, away from the sight of land. Most, however, choose to live in rural areas, such as grasslands, forests, and other wild places.

A large proportion of North America's bird species are migratory—that is, they do not spend the whole year in a single location—but instead move with the seasons to places more suited to their needs. Many spend the breeding season in the far north, taking advantage of a profusion of flying insects and a distinct lack of predators. Once the young have been fledged, they fly south before the onset of winter. Others, such as the hummingbird, remain in warmer areas, and overwinter in the tropics. Some, such as the Arctic tern make almost unbelievable journeys, flying from one pole to the other and back, in step with the seasons.

Across the world, there are about nine thousand different species of birds, with somewhere around eleven hundred species living in or visiting North America. These represent around twenty different orders and eighty different families, depending on exactly which species you include. Order is the rank in the classification of living things that lies below the classification of class—for birds Aves. Family is the classification between order and "genus." An order can contain several families—for example, in the order Falconiformes

PAGES 6–7: Sandhill Cranes can be easily identified in the air as they fly: Their necks are extended and they make more or less constant calls to one another, unlike herons, which fly with their necks tucked in and make only occasional sounds. Bosque Del Apache National Wildlife Reserve, New Mexico, USA.

LEFT: The Sandhill Crane is the most common crane species in the world. When it migrates, it gathers together in large numbers. Here such a concentration is waking up to a foggy morning at an important staging point on the Platte River, Nebraska, USA.

there are two families that occur in North America, the Accipitridae and the Falconidae. The former includes the hawks, kites, and eagles, of which there are 233 species worldwide, with twenty-eight being found in this region. The latter covers the caracaras and falcons, with sixty-two species worldwide and ten North American species. There is a third family within order Falconiformes—the Cathartidae; however, these are all South American birds.

The North American continent is blessed with a large number of different bird species. Some of these, such as the House Sparrow, have established themselves following either deliberate or accidental introductions. Others, such as the Cattle Egret, have made their own way across to the Americas by crossing the Atlantic Ocean from Africa; they now flourish in all the lower forty-eight states.

There are many different definitions as to exactly what constitutes a North American bird. The first list, which was published in 1886 by the American Ornithologists' Union (AOU), included those species that are found north of Mexico, but included Baja California, Bermuda, and Greenland. This situation was accepted for nearly a hundred years, but in 1983 Mexico was added, along with all of Central America as far south as Panama. The islands of the West Indies and Hawaii were also included, but Greenland was not. The American Birding Association (ABA) uses a different regime—it covers the forty-nine continental states and Canada, as well as the French islands of Saint-Pierre and Miquelon.

Human Involvement

The history of human involvement with the birds of North America can be divided into two time periods. The first of these can be considered to start when humans first moved to the continent some ten thousand or so years ago, just as the last Ice Age was coming to an end. It ended when European settlers arrived in the early 1500s. The second period is from that date to the present day. Not much is known about what effect the appearance of post-Ice Age Eurasian settlers had on the native bird populations; however, it is thought that they had a marked influence on the decline, and eventual extinction, of many large land mammals. These included such behemoths as the woolly mammoth, giant ground sloths, and the mastodon. It is entirely likely that their disappearance would have had corresponding effects on local habitats, and therefore may have contributed to the ability of some bird species to survive. When white Europeans settlers arrived some five hundred years ago, a new era began for the wildlife of the North American continent—sadly, almost all of it was bad. For the first couple of hundred years, these colonists struggled to survive, and as a result most of the continent remained unexplored. As more and more pioneers arrived, however, they spread out and began "taming" the land—for the most part this meant cutting down the forests for timber and plowing the earth to grow crops. As time went on this had more and more of an impact on the environment.

LEFT: The cypress swamps of Louisiana provide excellent habitats for Great Egrets, which thrive in the shallow waters that teem with wildlife. They wade slowly looking for prey and when they locate a suitable target, they lunge out and stab it with their sharp bills. Lake Martin, Louisiana, USA.

BELOW: While many birds have small, delicate beaks dedicated to pecking at small fragments of food, others have enormous beaks. The Brown Pelican, for instance, has a huge mouth that enables it to catch fish in open water, simply by engulfing them. Monterey Bay, California, USA.

The Passenger Pigeon

One of the best illustrations of just how wrong things went is the story of what happened to the Passenger Pigeon (*Ectopistes migratorius*). It was a graceful bird, with a long tail and blue feathers, that flew in vast flocks across much of the United States. It went from being one of the most numerous birds on the planet to extinction in only a couple of decades. It is thought that there were about 5 billion Passenger Pigeons when white settlers first arrived. There were many stories of how during their annual migration, they would block out the sun for hours on end, so great were their numbers. Unfortunately for them, they were considered to be good to eat, and their feathers were also in demand for decorative uses. As a result, the slaughter began. As late as the mid-1800s, there were still hundreds of millions to be seen—a single roosting site could measure five miles wide and twelve miles long. Nesting colonies were even bigger, with the largest one on record covering 850 square miles. At the time, people thought that they were so many of these fast-flying birds that the depredations would have little or no effect on their numbers. Consequently, they were killed in enormous numbers, a situation that was made possible by the new transportation networks opened up as the railroads became established. Many tens of millions a year were killed, but it was not long before the toll became unsustainable, and their populations began to crash. With a very low breeding rate, Passenger Pigeons were doomed from the start. To make matters worse, they relied on the country's extensive deciduous woodlands for the majority of their food. When these were cut down, the birds simply had nowhere to go, and it was not long before the large flocks were no longer seen. The last wild Passenger Pigeon died around 1900, and the last captive bird died in the Cincinnati Zoo in 1914.

Other Losses

The Passenger Pigeon is not the only bird to have been driven to extinction in modern times. Since white settlers arrived, at least two others have also been lost, the Labrador Duck (*Camptorhynchus labradorius*) and the Carolina Parakeet (*Conuropsis carolinensis*). It is also likely that Bachman's Warbler (*Vermivora bachmanii*) is no longer extant, because no living specimens have been seen for nearly twenty years. It is thought that the Labrador Duck spent the winter along the Atlantic Coast of North America, where it fed on shellfish and crustaceans sifted from shallow water and silt. They probably bred on the coast of Labrador and other areas to the north. During breeding season, the males had striking black-and-white plumage, whereas the females and juveniles were a brown-gray color with a white wing patch. Sadly, the details will never be confirmed because the species disappeared before its natural history was fully documented. It is thought that the last one was seen at Elmira, New York, in 1878. In many ways, it is still a mystery as to why this lovely bird was lost. Although many were shot by hunters, it is likely that several other factors such as ecological changes were responsible for its ultimate demise.

The Carolina Parakeet

At one time, the Carolina Parakeet was the only species of parrot that was found in mainland North America north of Mexico. It was a medium-sized bird with a green body, a yellow head, and orange markings around its beak. It lived in large, noisy flocks in deciduous forests and along the edges of forests across much of the eastern United States. Under natural conditions, it lived on a diet composed of native fruits and seeds. When large areas of the countryside were converted to agriculture, however, it soon became a serious pest to the growers of cultivated fruit and grain. Consequently, it was branded as a pest species and enormous numbers were killed in a short space of time. The fact that it had highly decorative feathers only made matters worse because they were in huge demand from the hat-making trade. By the late 1860s range of the Carolina Parakeet was restricted to Florida, and it was officially listed as extinct by the 1920s.

The Eskimo Curlew

The Eskimo Curlew (*Numenius borealis*) used to be a very common bird—up until the 1870s, enormous flocks used to migrate across parts of Canada and the United States to and from their summer grounds in the Alaskan and Canadian Arctic. As winter approached, they gorged themselves on the berries of various tundra shrubs until they had built up sufficient fat reserves. They then left for a prolonged journey out over the Atlantic Ocean and down across the equator as far as South America. The return journey in the spring was made in April and May, when they stopped off in the Great Plains, where they gained sustenance from the large numbers of Rocky Mountain grasshoppers found in the long prairie grasses. In the late 1800s Eskimo Curlew populations came under extreme pressure from many directions. Most of the native grasslands of the Great Plains were converted to agricultural, wiping out the insects on which these birds depended during a vital part of their migration cycle. On top of this, Eskimo Curlew meat became a primary substitute for the dwindling Passenger Pigeon. Market hunters, along with increasing numbers of sport hunters, took a heavy toll. The curlew's numbers plummeted to such a degree that it was thought to be extinct by the early 1900s, though the last known individual was collected in 1963. Occasional unconfirmed sightings suggest that there may be a small breeding population, but it is still listed as an endangered species and some authorities consider the Eskimo Curlew extinct.

The Ivory-billed Woodpecker

One bird that was considered to be extinct—but apparently is not—is the Ivory-billed Woodpecker (*Campephilus principalis*). For more than sixty years, no living specimens had been seen, and so it was thought to be lost forever. In February 2004, however, a single individual was spotted in the Cache River National Wildlife Refuge in Arkansas. Some experts questioned the veracity of this sighting, but it was such an important matter that Cornell Laboratory of Ornithology

and The Nature Conservancy initiated a study project. More than fifty experts committed to a yearlong survey, and it was with great delight that they were able to report multiple sightings over this period. This was heralded as a great success, and although not everyone is convinced that the case has been proven, it has provided the impetus for a massive Ivory-billed Woodpecker conservation project in the area.

Conservation—The Success Stories

These days, people are very much more environmentally aware, and large numbers of them belong to or support conservation groups across the world. These organizations have helped turn around the fortunes of some of our rarest birds. Examples include the California Condor, Peregrine Falcon, Whooping Crane, and the Wood Duck. Such birds are often among the first creatures in an ecosystem to visibly suffer when the local environment comes under pressure by anything from over-grazing to heavy-metal pollution.

RIGHT: A lot of bird species form themselves into flocks—they may do so to roost, to migrate, for mate selection purposes, or simply to forage. Whatever the reasons, there is security in numbers—it is far harder for a predator to approach a group of birds without being seen than it is to approach an individual bird. Here a group of pigeons gather on telephone wires. Utah, USA.

BELOW: The eggs of most passerines are colored, unlike those of other birds, which tend to be white. There are exceptions to this rule, especially among some ground-nesting birds that produce eggs with cryptic patterns or colors for camouflage. This is the nest of a Red-winged Blackbird. Whatcom County, Washington, USA.

PAGES 14–15: The Venice Area Audubon Rookery encompasses a small wooded island in the middle of a Florida lake. It is home to a wide variety of birds including Great White Egrets, Great Blue Herons, Anhingas, and Black-crowned Night-Herons. Venice, Florida, USA.

RIGHT: This freeze-frame image of a Northern Cardinal slowing down to land shows just how a bird's feathers interact. Note how the wing and tail feathers have all spread out to present the maximum surface area—this is so that they can develop the maximum braking effect.

PAGE 18: The male Northern Cardinal (*Cardinalis cardinalis*) is easily identifiable by its bright red color, crest, and black beak surround. Common in the east of the country and as far south as Central America, the Northern Cardinal is a winter resident whose range is moving northward. It has also been introduced to Hawaii. Edinburg, Texas, USA.

PAGE 19: The Blue Jay is common backyard visitor east of the Rocky Mountains. It may be beautiful, but it's not quiet, announcing its presence with a variety of vocalizations, including whistles, rattles, and the familiar shrill call in which it seems to scream its name. Lincoln, Nebraska, USA.

The California Condor

California Condors (*Gymnogyps californanus*) are among North America's largest and most impressive birds. They are found in California and Arizona and in Mexico's Baja California. They use their incredible wingspan—more than 9 feet in some cases—to soar over the countryside as they search for the carrion on which they feed. In doing so, they can cover enormous distances—150 miles a day is not uncommon. Unfortunately for these magnificent birds, their feeding habits leave them dangerously exposed to a series of environmental problems. Being carrion eaters, they are adapted to feed solely from dead animals—they cannot catch and kill their own food—and are exposed to carcasses that contain dangerous toxins, either because the animals were poisoned in the name of pest control or had built up large amounts of pesticides in their bodies or had high lead content after being struck by shotgun pellets. It is no surprise that for many years, the survival of the California Condor looked to be in serious doubt.

In the early 1980s, a large captive breeding program was initiated and all the remaining wild condors were trapped. Two breeding programs were started—one at San Diego Wild Animal Park and one at Los Angeles Zoo. In 1994, when enough young birds were available, a third program was started at the World Center for Birds of Prey. By carefully coordinating the blood lines of the various birds, these three organizations have managed to ensure the highest possible amount of genetic diversity, thus increasing the condor's chance of long-term survival. The programs have been extremely successful, and reintroduction to the wild began in 1991. It has continued to this day, and their numbers have gone from a low of fewer than thirty individuals to a present day population of nearly 300. The wild birds still face threats from a number of directions—these include deaths from collisions with power lines, and the ever-present risk of illegal hunting and lead poisoning. Sadly, it will be a significant amount of time before the wild populations are able to sustain themselves, and until then more captive-bred birds will have to be released periodically.

The Wood Duck

The Wood Duck (*Aix sponsa*) is another North American bird species that suffered at the hands of an expanding human population in the nineteenth century. At that time, many thought the duck might become extinct because of over-hunting and habitat loss. Fortunately, tough game laws protected them from hunting for many years and today, thanks to enormous conservation efforts—largely by the hunters themselves—the Wood Duck is distributed across a wider range than ever before. One of the main factors in the Wood Duck's recovery is its high reproduction rate—a single clutch can contain up to fourteen eggs. Many birds also lay multiple clutches, often in other individual's nests.

The Whooping Crane

The Whooping Crane (*Grus americana*) was never a common species, and by the time that hunting and a loss of its prairie marsh habitat had taken its toll, it became a very rare bird indeed. By the 1940s, only sixteen cranes overwintered on the Texan coast. Fortunately, action was taken in time, and huge conservation efforts have led to their numbers increasing significantly, and now there are more than 360 wild birds. Saving the Whooping Crane involved getting official protection for their breeding, migration, and overwintering sites, in addition to launching a series of captive breeding programs. During the 1990s, the only wild population was breeding in the Wood Buffalo National Park in Canada's Northwest Territories. The birds then flew south to overwinter in the Aransas National Wildlife Refuge in Texas. It had been known for some time that a second migrating colony was needed in order for the species to have any chance of a long-term survival, and so a plan was put together to establish one. In 2001, a group of eight juveniles were introduced to the existing birds in Florida in the hope that a migratory flock could be established. In order to teach them where to go, they were trained to follow a ultralight aircraft. When they were ready to leave, they were led on a well-publicized journey all the way from their home in the Necedah National Wildlife Refuge in Wisconsin to Florida's Chassahowitska National Wildlife Refuge, where they overwintered. The following spring, five of the birds flew north, making all the efforts worthwhile. It is hoped that the success of this project will lead to other migrating colonies being established elsewhere.

The American Peregrine Falcon

The Peregrine Falcon (*Falco pergrinus*) is a classic example of how a species was nearly lost for all time, but saved by government action. In the 1960s, pesticide residues had built up in the falcon's wild population to such an extent that few birds were able to breed successfully—and none were found anywhere in the eastern United States. This was mainly due to the pesticide DDT. When it was first developed, it was hailed as a savior for agriculture; however, no one realized what long-term exposure would do to the environment. After considerable research, scientists were able to prove a direct link between DDT and eggshell thinning, and in 1972, the use of DDT was banned. At this time several major conservation efforts were initiated, including captive breeding and release programs, and the numbers of Peregrine Falcons slowly began to recover. In 1999 their populations had grown to the point where the falcon was removed from the endangered species list.

Conservation—Issues For The Future

There are many issues that need to be addressed if the progress made by conservation bodies is to continue. The main threats to birds include continued habitat loss, as well as reducing the number killed by illegal hunting, poisoning, and trapping. On a much smaller scale,

it is also necessary to reduce the number of birds killed accidentally by mankind's day-to-day activities. For example, in the 1970s significant numbers of dead owls were found lying along the sides of roads; however, it was unclear exactly how they died. Examination showed that they had not experienced direct motor vehicle impacts. Consequently, a number of ornithologists began to study the matter carefully. Their observations eventually came up with a surprising conclusion. Owls are nocturnal predators, and their habit of flying along roadsides to hunt for small rodents left them dangerously exposed to collision injuries from the long radio antennas that became fashionable on cars back then. Fortunately for the owl population, whip antennas went out of fashion as quickly as they had come in, and the issue more or less went away on its own.

Another illustration of the unintentional killing of birds is the number of raptors that are killed every year by electricity lines. The problem is that the poles erected to support power lines are also attractive perches for many kinds of birds. The smaller species are largely unaffected; however, the much greater wingspan of the bigger birds of prey, such as eagles and hawks, means that they sometimes are able to touch two lines at the same time. When this happens, they can be electrocuted in milliseconds. The problem appears to be mainly linked to older grid networks, where the power lines are close enough for this to happen—modern networks are more widely spaced. Many of the power companies concerned have done their best to try and reduce these deaths or even eliminate them altogether. One method has been to install special perches above the poles that incorporate guards to prevent the birds from getting too close to the wires. In many areas this has been very successful; however, it is an ongoing issue and academic research work continues—often funded by the power companies themselves.

Global Warming

Although human-caused bird deaths—be they deliberate or accidental—are very sad, they pale into insignificance when compared to the threat from global warming. This is one of the greatest challenges mankind—indeed, the entire planet—has yet had to face. It must be recognized, though, that the complete picture as to why the Earth's temperatures have risen significantly over the last fifty years is still not clear. The easiest solution is simply to blame everything on global industrialization; however, we ignore other potential factors at our own peril. No one knows, for instance, what effects increases in radiation from the sun over the same period are having. While scientists all over the world are working to establish the full story, others are documenting the effects that the warming is having. These range from the bleaching of coral reefs near the equator, to the melting of the polar ice caps. This, in turn, has a further consequence—as the ice melts, the sea levels rise. In the long term, many countries will be devastated by flooding. Others will simply cease to exist. In the meantime, the geographical distribution of many animal species has already changed. A lot of birds,

for instance, no longer visit their traditional haunts. This is especially true of marshland species, since their habitats are particularly sensitive to environmental changes.

In Alaska, many seabirds such as the Black Guillemot are under threat because the reduction in pack ice coverage has forced them to fly farther afield to nest and feed. Farther south, the changes in ocean temperatures have also altered the levels of fish stocks. This has had a dramatic effect on species like the Sooty Shearwater, which has seen serious population crashes in recent years. On the other hand, some species are actually benefiting from the changes. It has been shown, for instance, that the Mexican Jay is now breeding, on average, nearly two weeks earlier in the season than it did only thirty years ago.

Habitat Loss and Conservation

North America is home to a fantastic array of different habitats and wild places. These range from rivers and lakes to marshes, mountains, and deserts. Bordering the oceans are rugged cliff-lined coasts, as well as sandy beaches and coral reefs. While all of these have their own diverse spectrums of plants and animals, they share a common threat—that of habitat loss due to human activities. Although the general public is now far better educated about this, it takes more than widespread goodwill to deal with the problem. While there are usually various short-term fixes, such as reducing local pollution, reversing wetland drainage, and so on, these risk being a waste of time if a sustainable regime is not identified. Probably the best method of achieving success is by directly involving local economies in the conservation efforts. This can be done, for instance, by setting up ecotourism so the wild areas generate income for the people who live there. They then have a vested interest in ensuring that the wildlife is fostered year in, year out.

When the decision has been made to restore a habitat to its former condition, there is a lot more to it than simply finding the money, manpower and equipment. Before any action is taken, it is necessary to perform an in-depth study of the area, so that the local ecosystem is sufficiently well understood to enable its long-term management. Some forests, for instance, rely on regular fires—without them, many trees are unable to establish seedlings. A much more serious aspect, however, is that without regular managed burning, the dry underbrush can build up to dangerous levels. Should this "fuel" catch fire, it burns so fiercely that the high temperatures generated kill everything. This can leave vast areas denuded of any significant plant or animal life for years to come. With care and forethought, though, it is possible to find ways that allow both the wildlife and local industries—such as forestry and agriculture, to prosper.

It is not possible for habitat conservation to be really successful, however, unless the efforts extend to cover the full geographical range of the species being conserved. It would be futile, for instance, to try

LEFT: Birds that feed on small insects and fragments of vegetation need to be able to forage with great precision. Consequently, they need to have short, thin bills, as can be seen on this White-Breasted Nuthatch. McLeansville, North Carolina, USA.

RIGHT: The bill of a bird that eats large amounts of seeds or nuts needs to be strong enough to crack them open. The short, sturdy bill on a Tufted Titmouse, shown foraging in a shallow puddle, is perfect for hammering open seed hulls. McLeansville, North Carolina, USA.

and restore an endangered bird's breeding ground, if its overwintering sites were not also conserved. It is therefore vital that international boundaries do not get in the way. Consequently, policy coordination often has to be done at a geopolitical level—this is why bird conservation groups need all the support they can get. This can vary from simply becoming a member of a recognized ornithological society to taking part in organized surveys of species or habitats. Before any significant influence can be exerted, it is necessary to document what is going on so that the best practices can be developed. Should it be noticed that a particular population of birds has begun to decline, for instance, then the causes can be identified and the most practical solutions implemented. The knowledge can then be used to guide everyone from politicians to conservation workers.

Birdwatching

Birdwatching is a rewarding pastime for people of all ages. For youngsters it is an excellent introduction to the joys of the outdoor world, whereas for those of more advanced years it is something that can even be enjoyed from behind a window. Every facet of the subject has its fascinations, from learning the different kinds of bird songs to finding out how to distinguish specific species by the coloration of particular feathers. On top of this, there is the fact that many birds are migratory, so the mix of species we see around us changes throughout the year. These days there are many sources of information on the subject, ranging from books to videos, CD/DVDs, television programs, and, of course, the Internet. There are thousands of excellent websites, many of which have illustrated guides to help you identify the birds you have seen. If you have a camera, you may wish to start building up a photographic record of what you have seen. A good image is probably the best way to confirm a sighting. One of the great advantages of this is that if you are unsure of your identification, it easy to email your digital photos to someone else for an expert opinion. Learning how to distinguish between different bird calls is also a great aid in determining which species is which. Some websites have short sound clips for the different kinds of birds. These can be listened to at the click of the mouse, making it easy to compare the calls of similar species. It should be noted that males, females, and juveniles of the same species may make calls that are quite unlike one another, and that they may also change significantly depending on the time of year—especially during the breeding season.

Feeding Wild Birds

One of the best ways to watch wild birds—and help them at the same time—is to feed them in your own yard. This gives you the chance to monitor which species are in the area, as well as how many of them there are. Something close to half of the households in the United States provide food for birds at least part of the time, so it is clearly a major source of nutrition for those species that visit feeders. This

especially true during the winter, when food can be hard to come by. There are many different kinds of feeders available these days, and many stores stock a good variety of nuts, seeds, suet, and other suitable foodstuffs. If you would like to put food out, but are unsure which kinds to buy, the best thing is to try a few of each type, and see what the birds in your area like the most. Feeding birds household leftovers is generally discouraged—some contain ingredients, such as unacceptably high levels of salt or sugar, which are inappropriate for bird diets. It should also be noted that easy access to clean water is vitally important when the temperatures are very low, as birds need to drink often. If all the natural sources are frozen, they will die very quickly.

Birdwatching Organizations
Many organizations exist for the eager birding enthusiast. These collect and collate the data recorded by serious observers, and often have informative websites and lively Internet chat rooms. Some, such as the American Ornithologists' Union, are aimed at professionals; however, there are many others that are more suited to the amateur. For more information on various organizations, see the list at the end of the book.

LEFT: The difference in height between a Great Blue Heron and a Herring Gull is clearly evident in this scene. The heron's long legs allow it to hunt in much deeper water than if they were the same length as those of the gull. Fort Myers Beach, Florida, USA.

RIGHT: The relationship between some plants and birds is so direct that many depend on each other for survival. The structure of certain flowers is so unusual that sometimes only one species of bird is able to pollinate it. Likewise, the bird may only be able to feed from that one kind of flower. Consequently, if either species dies out, so does the other. Arizona, USA.

FAR RIGHT: Many wetland habitats are under threat from pollution, commercial development or agricultural "improvement." As can be seen here, such places can be a haven for a wide variety of waterfowl species, especially those that migrate over long distances, and so their protection is of paramount importance. California, USA.

PAGE 26: Like many other species of birds, Tundra Swans migrate to and from their breeding grounds every year, when they fly in the "V" formation characteristic of geese and swans.

PAGE 27: Some birds, such as this Broad-Billed Hummingbird, have evolved to feed from very specific nutritional sources. In this example, it has developed a long, thin bill and an even longer tongue so that it can gather nectar efficiently from flowers with long, thin shapes. Arizona, USA.

RIGHT: When large birds such as Canada Geese take flight, they often do so in "vee" formations. Recent work by scientists has shown that this grouping gives the best aerodynamic efficiency for all but the lead bird. The following birds all gain lift from the one in front.

PAGE 30: The ground-feeding Whooping Crane has a long, sharp bill that it uses for a variety of purposes, including stabbing at fast-moving animals such as fish, frogs and insects, as well as for pecking at vegetative matter or probing soft mud for crustaceans.

PAGE 31: Some species, such as these Canada Geese, gather together in large flocks to overwinter. While this can be a wonderful sight for onlookers, it can also be a real problem for local farmers because significant numbers of large birds can do a lot of damage to crops. Wapusk National Park, Manitoba, Canada.

LEFT: Geese tend to overwinter in flocks—this affords them a degree of protection due to the "strength in numbers" principle, but also allows them to socialize. This group has chosen to settle on a rocky outcrop. Wapusk National Park, Manitoba, Canada.

ABOVE: The Great Blue Heron is a solitary hunter, since it is an ambush specialist—being a patient stalker is the best way to catch fast-moving prey like fish in the eddies and currents of rivers and streams. Great Falls, Potomac River, Maryland, USA.

LEFT: Many birds like to construct their nests in holes in trees because they afford a great deal of protection against predators. Some birds find and occupy disused holes, whereas others, such as the Red-shafted Flicker seen here, dig out their own. USA

RIGHT: Birdwatching is a very popular pastime the world over. Many people like to feed birds at home, and although feeders containing nuts or seeds are the most common, there are also many others ways to feed them. This Downy Woodpecker, for instance, is eating a peanut butter mix that has been put into a hole in a tree. McLeansville, North Carolina, USA.

PAGE 36: During the breeding season, many birds can be very aggressive—in the early part of the season the males of some species will attack and even kill other males that attempt to invade their territory. Once a nest has been built, however, it is common for both parents to drive off potential predators or competitors. Here a Wood Duck charges an unwanted intruder.

PAGE 37: When nestlings gather together like these owl chicks, it is mainly to enable them to conserve heat. If their body temperatures fall too low, they will sicken and die, and so this is an important behavioral response. Wapusk National Park, Manitoba, Canada.

LEFT: This image shows the red mouth of a Great Gray Owl chick—it has been shown that when parent birds see this coloration, it stimulates them to feed their young. In this species, the food is primarily small animals such as rodents.

RIGHT: When a bird such as this Great Egret eats a fish whole, it always swallows it head-first. This is to avoid the fish's spines from catching in its throat—a situation that could injure or even kill it. Venice, Florida, USA.

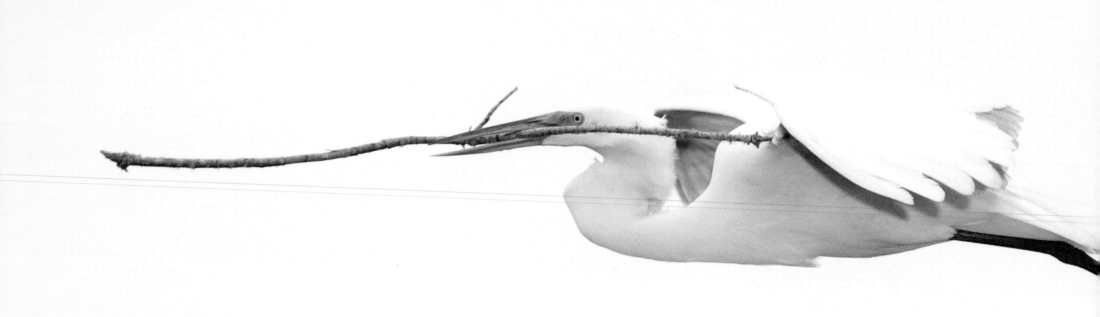

ABOVE: Before any eggs can be laid, a nest is needed. Some birds, such as cuckoos, lay theirs in with the eggs of other species. Others, such as starlings often simply evict the rightful owners and move in. The vast majority, however, build their own—some do so from scratch, whereas others may add to a nest that is left over from the previous season. Here a Great Egret can be seen carrying a stick to its nest. St. Augustine, Florida, USA.

RIGHT: Although the Burrowing Owl is often seen hunting by day, it also hunts throughout the night. In order to do so—like the other members of the family—it has evolved very large eyes. This gives it the ability to see in low-light conditions. Cape Coral, Florida, USA.

FAR LEFT: While some parent birds are stimulated to feed their young when they see the nestling's red mouth lining, the same response in others is triggered in different ways. Some seagulls, for instance, are encouraged to do so when their chicks peck at their bill. It is an innate response for the chicks of these species to peck at anything red—such as the red spot seen on this bird's bill. La Jolla, California, USA.

LEFT: When the Brown Pelican is on land, it can look very ungainly. However, when it is diving—as can be seen here—it is quite clear that the pelican is supremely adapted for its ecological niche. Huntington Beach, California, USA.

PAGE 44: Courtship is an important part of the breeding season for many birds. The rituals and displays help in the mate selection process. For some species, these involve complicated dance routines—with others, it is a much simpler affair. This is a Great Egret showing off its long plumes which are known as "aigrettes." Florida, USA.

PAGE 45: The talons on Ferruginous Hawks are powerful and very sharp. This helps them seize and kill their prey, hunted over open ground, which can be anything from prairie grasslands to desert areas. They mostly take small animals such as ground squirrels, prairie dogs and rabbits.

LEFT: The Great Blue Heron, like the other members of its family, uses its sharp beak in a sudden stabbing motion to lunge through shallow water to catch its prey. This may be anything from frogs to fish. Unfortunately, herons often take ornamental fish from backyard ponds, which can make them unpopular with homeowners. Florida, USA.

RIGHT: The Dunlin, like many other shorebirds migrates to the extreme north of the continent to breed on the Arctic tundra. One reason for this is that there are unimaginable numbers of insects for them to feed on, which makes it easy to feed their nestlings. Wapusk National Park, Manitoba, Canada.

PAGE 48: While a particular habitat conservation project may be targeted at protecting a specific species of bird, the whole spectrum of other animals and plants in that area is likely to benefit too. Here a deer grazes alongside a small bird in the Grand Teton National Park, Wyoming, USA.

PAGE 49: The Northern Bobwhite, which is a popular quarry with hunters, is a small game bird that is resident from the Great Lakes down into Central America. Across this range there are around twenty-two different subspecies, some of which are more distinctively plumed than others. Hidalgo County, Texas, USA.

RIGHT: California Condors feed exclusively on carrion—in order to do so, they are equipped with large talons and a beak that is specially adapted to rip meat off carcasses. They can be very aggressive toward other birds that attempt to share their meal, and will chase them off—with the exception of Golden Eagles, which are left well alone.

RIGHT: The Sharp-Tailed Grouse is a medium to large game bird that is found in a wide variety of open country habitats. Its range extends from Alaska in the north, across Cañada, and down into Colorado in the south. Dinosaur National Monument, Utah, USA.

ABOVE: The Osprey is a magnificent bird of prey that feeds almost entirely on fish. It has specially adapted talons that help it to maintain a grip on the fish it captures. It is one of the largest raptors in North America, with a wingspan that can reach to more than 70 inches (180 cm).

RIGHT: The Mourning Dove is abundant across most of North America from central Canada to Panama. It feeds in small flocks or pairs on the ground where it eats various vegetative matter. The bulk of its diet, however, is composed of seeds. Lincoln, Nebraska, USA.

LEFT: The American Avocet used to be hunted extensively; however, it has since been designated as a protected species. This has led to a population increase, but threats still remain— habitat degradation and destruction of their breeding and wintering grounds continues to be a problem. Montana, USA.

RIGHT: Also known as the "Mexican Eagle," the Crested Caracara is a long-legged falcon of open country, where it feeds on carrion. It is primarily a bird of the tropics, and so is only found in the extreme southern reaches of the United States. Its range extends from there down into central South America. Linn, Texas, USA.

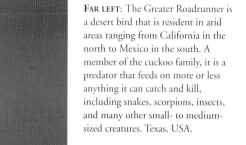

FAR LEFT: The Greater Roadrunner is a desert bird that is resident in arid areas ranging from California in the north to Mexico in the south. A member of the cuckoo family, it is a predator that feeds on more or less anything it can catch and kill, including snakes, scorpions, insects, and many other small- to medium-sized creatures. Texas, USA.

LEFT: In this image of a Snail Kite taking flight, the primary feathers can be seen clearly. They spread out like extended fingers at the tips of each wing, and help generate the massive lift required for a bird of this size to become airborne. Osceola County, Florida, USA.

LEFT: Once the Bald Eagle has reached a sufficient altitude, it sets its wings to produce the optimum gliding characteristics. In this way, it can cover the greatest amount of ground in the search for food, and yet expend the minimum amount of energy.

PAGE 60: The Bald Eagle, scientific name *Haliaeetus leucocephalus,* has a powerful beak that it uses effectively when eating its prey. These beautiful birds pair up for life—in the breeding season they build a nest in a tall tree, where the female lays between one and three eggs. Mount Rainier National Park, Washington, USA.

PAGE 61: This image of a Bald Eagle swooping in to catch a fish shows the complex arrangement of different wing feathers. In this position, it is creating the maximum possible aerodynamic braking so that it can approach its prey at high speed—and yet slow down enough to be able to actually catch it. Kachemak Bay, Alaska, USA.

RIGHT: Many shorebirds have long, thin bills—these provide a particularly efficient means of finding and catching small animals by probing in shallow water and soft mud. Here a Long-Billed Curlew has captured a fiddler crab. Fort DeSoto Park, Florida, USA.

FAR RIGHT: Brewer's Blackbird is a communal bird with an iridescent blue-green sheen to its feathers. It inhabits open grassy areas where it feeds on plant material such as berries, seeds, and fruits, as well as small invertebrates such as insects and worms.

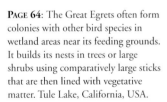

PAGE 64: The Great Egrets often form colonies with other bird species in wetland areas near its feeding grounds. It builds its nests in trees or large shrubs using comparatively large sticks that are then lined with vegetative matter. Tule Lake, California, USA.

PAGE 65: All the captive-bred California Condors that have been released back into the wild have been tagged with large numbers so that observers can monitor their well-being from a distance. This juvenile bird is sunning itself on the South Rim of the Grand Canyon. Arizona, USA.

Birds of Prey

Birds of prey, which are also known as raptors, are birds that hunt for their food by using their curved beaks and sharp talons. North America is home to a wide range of these wonderful birds, including eagles, owls, hawks, and vultures. Some, such as the Bald Eagle are well known the world over; however, there are many other species that are far less easily recognized. Although many are flourishing as species, sadly, several have suffered from serious decline in recent years. There are many causes for this—habitat loss is a major factor, but the use of persistent pesticides such as the now-banned DDT also took a terrible toll for many years. The California Condor, for instance, came close to extinction—a situation that was only made worse by its very low reproduction rate. Many of these impressive birds were also illegally shot, and in the mid to late 1980s the authorities decided that things had gone too far. In desperation, the few surviving wild individuals were caught and put into special breeding programs run by the San Diego Wild Animal Park and Los Angeles Zoo. The incredible efforts invested into this project paid off, and in the last few years young captive-bred birds have been released back into the wild in Southern California and at the Grand Canyon.

Bald Eagles used to be very common birds right across North America—when European settlers first arrived, it is thought that there were more than half a million of them. Since then, however, their numbers plummeted to less than 500 pairs in the 1960s. Large numbers were simply shot for fun, whereas others were poisoned either deliberately or by agricultural chemicals or environmental pollution. Conservationists have put a vast amount of work into reversing this trend, and as a result, the Bald Eagle is once again making a return to the American landscape. These efforts have been backed up by strict environmental protection laws, including the Endangered Species Act of 1973, the Bald Eagle Protection Act of 1940, the Migratory Bird Treaty Act of 1918, and the Lacey Act.

The North American birds of prey can be divided into six main groups—these are the owls, hawks, eagles, falcons, vultures, and condors. Although most owls are primarily night fliers, some species such as the Snowy Owl are diurnal—that is, active during the day. The smallest is the Elf Owl, which grows to a maximum weight of only one and a half ounces, and a height of between five and six inches. The largest American bird of prey is the California Condor, with a wingspan of around 108 inches (2.74 m) and a weight of between 17 and 22 lbs. (7-10 kg). The condor is not the largest North American bird, though—the Trumpeter Swan grows both longer and heavier, and the American White Pelican can have a greater wingspan. Turkey Vultures, on the other hand, are only half the size of the condor, giving you an idea of their exceptional size.

Year Round
Summer (breeding)
Winter (non-breeding)
Migration

LEFT: Bald Eagles are migratory, moving south as winter approaches and then north again in the spring. They travel at around 30mph, always return to the same places—both at their over-wintering spots and in their nesting grounds.

LEFT INSET: Range of the Bald Eagle.

ABOVE: The Bald Eagle was designated as the U.S. national bird in 1782, and since then proud Americans have used its image for all types of patriotic expression. The characteristic white markings do not appear until the bird is between four and six years old. Colorado, USA.

PAGE 68: Although Bald Eagles catch fish, they will take waterfowl and small mammals when the opportunity arises. They are also fond of carrion; however, if there is nothing else to eat, they will search the shoreline for crabs, clams, sea urchins, and other edible creatures. Aleutian Islands, Alaska, USA.

PAGE 69: The Bald Eagle is a very long-lived creature. In the wild, healthy birds can live for up to forty years, provided they manage to avoid illegal hunters. Captive specimens have survived for longer than this—there are records of one individual reaching the incredible age of sixty.

LEFT: The Ferruginous Hawk is a large, broad-winged, broad-tailed bird with a wingspan of around 54 inches. It lives in grassland areas where its diet is primarily made up of small mammals, however it will also take birds, reptiles, amphibians, and insects when the opportunity arises. Utah, USA.

LEFT INSET: Range of the Ferruginous Hawk.

Year Round

Summer (breeding)

Winter (non-breeding)

Migration

Year Round

Summer (breeding)

Winter (non-breeding)

Migration

Year Round

Summer (breeding)

Winter (non-breeding)

Migration

RIGHT: The Great Gray Owl is a very large predatory bird that has a wingspan of around 60 inches. It has a hooked beak, large yellow eyes, and a gray facial disc that is marked with characteristic dark rings. It hunts at night for a variety of small animals.

BELOW: The range of the Great Gray Owl.

- Year Round
- Summer (breeding)
- Winter (non-breeding)
- Migration

FAR RIGHT: The predominantly white coloration of the Snowy Owl helps it to blend in with the background landscape in winter. This gives it an advantage when hunting, as well as a degree of camouflage against would-be predators. Churchill, Manitoba, Canada.

LEFT: The Burrowing Owl is highly unusual in that it collects animal dung to place in and around its nest hole to attract dung beetles, which are a particular dietary favorite of this small owl. Marlo Island, Florida, USA.

RIGHT: As its name would suggest, the Burrowing Owl nests in holes in the ground. While it is more than capable of digging its own, it will readily take over existing holes that have been made by other animals, such as rabbits, prairie dogs, skunks, or armadillos.

BELOW: The range of the Burrowing Owl.

Year Round

Summer (breeding)

Winter (non-breeding)

Migration

LEFT: The Great Horned Owl is a very large bird that is easily distinguished by its long ear tufts. It has a wingspan of around 55 inches, yellow eyes, and a dark beak. It primarily hunts small mammals, but will also take birds, reptiles, and amphibians if the opportunity arises. Colorado, USA.

BELOW: The range of the Great Horned Owl.

Year Round
Summer (breeding)
Winter (non-breeding)
Migration

RIGHT: The Barn Owl is a large nocturnal predator with a wingspan of around 44 inches. It is found in grassland and agricultural areas, where it hunts for small animals, with rodents being a mainstay. The bird's name comes from the fact that it often nests in farm buildings.

RIGHT INSET: The range of the Barn Owl.

Year Round
Summer (breeding)
Winter (non-breeding)
Migration

RIGHT: The Northern Hawk Owl is a diurnal predator with a large head and yellow eyes. It can be distinguished from other owls by its long tail, and from hawks by the rounded shape of its head. Its diet mainly consists of small mammals and birds. Denali National Park, Alaska, USA.

BELOW: The range of the Northern Hawk Owl.

Year Round

Summer (breeding)

Winter (non-breeding)

Migration

RIGHT: Great Gray Owls make their nests at the top of dead trees. Sometimes they build their own; however, they will also take over ones that have been abandoned by other birds. The chicks are born with their eyes closed, and therefore need a great deal of care from their parents if they are to fledge successfully.

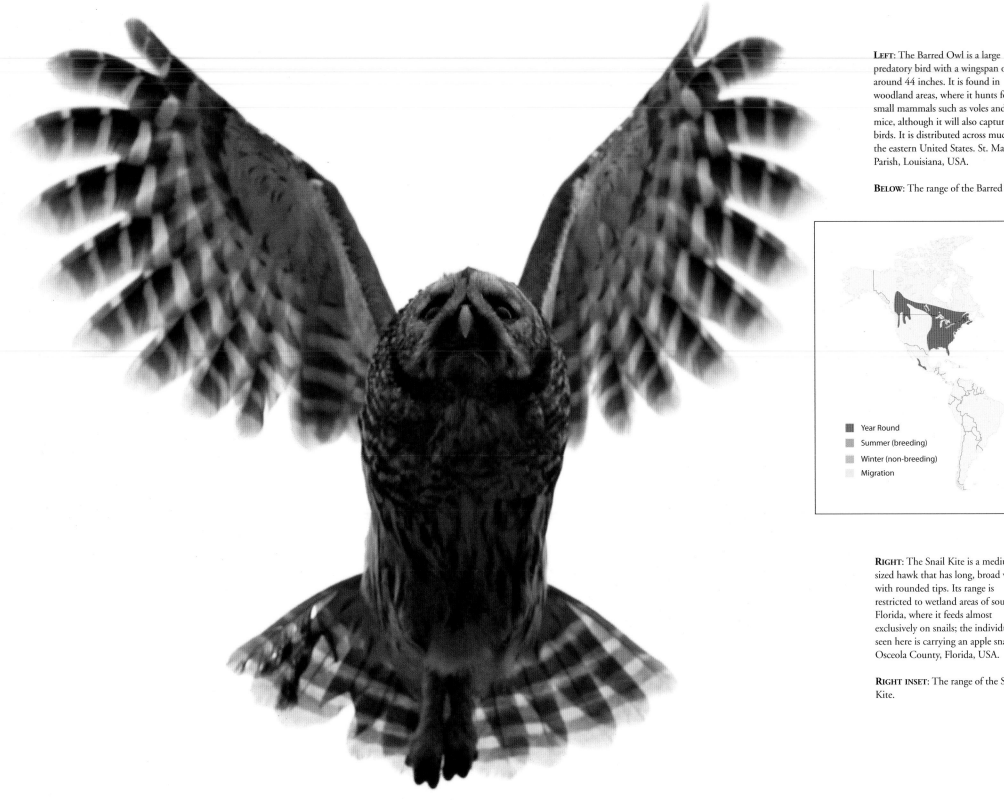

LEFT: The Barred Owl is a large predatory bird with a wingspan of around 44 inches. It is found in woodland areas, where it hunts for small mammals such as voles and mice, although it will also capture birds. It is distributed across much of the eastern United States. St. Martin Parish, Louisiana, USA.

BELOW: The range of the Barred Owl.

Year Round

Summer (breeding)

Winter (non-breeding)

Migration

RIGHT: The Snail Kite is a medium-sized hawk that has long, broad wings with rounded tips. Its range is restricted to wetland areas of southern Florida, where it feeds almost exclusively on snails; the individual seen here is carrying an apple snail. Osceola County, Florida, USA.

RIGHT INSET: The range of the Snail Kite.

Year Round
Summer (breeding)
Winter (non-breeding)
Migration

Year Round

Summer (breeding)

Winter (non-breeding)

Migration

Year Round
Summer (breeding)
Winter (non-breeding)
Migration

Year Round

Summer (breeding)

Winter (non-breeding)

Migration

LEFT: The Red-Shouldered Hawk has large, broad wings and a fairly long tail and lives in woodland areas. It feeds mainly on small mammals and birds; however—as can be seen with this individual that has caught a small snake—they will also take reptiles and amphibians. Indian Lake Estates, Florida, USA.

LEFT INSET: The range of the Red-Shouldered Hawk.

RIGHT: The Crested Caracara is a medium-sized, broad-winged hawk that is found in southern Texas. It has long legs and a long tail, as well as a hooked beak with which it will happily feed on carrion. It will, however, also hunt for birds, reptiles, and amphibians. Linn, Texas, USA.

BELOW: The range of the Crested Caracara.

- ▪ Year Round
- ▪ Summer (breeding)
- ▪ Winter (non-breeding)
- ▫ Migration

LEFT: Snowy Owls are large diurnal (day-flying) birds with a powerful flight. They are found in the Arctic; however, when there is insufficient food, large numbers move south into southern Canada and the northern United States. Their main prey is snowshoe hares, rodents, birds, and fish. Barrow, Alaska, USA.

RIGHT: The Eastern Screech Owl is a small, nocturnal, predatory bird that has distinctive ear tufts. There are three color types—gray, red, and brown—which really form a continuum of variation. The species is found in woodland areas, where it has a wide choice of diet consisting of insects, reptiles, amphibians, small mammals, or birds. Rio Grande City, Texas, USA.

BELOW: The range of the Eastern Screech Owl.

■ Year Round
■ Summer (breeding)
■ Winter (non-breeding)
■ Migration

PAGE 88: The Osprey is a large, narrow-winged hawk with a wingspan of around 54 inches, a white cap, and a short, hooked beak. They nest most frequently in wetlands. Not surprisingly, fish—caught by hovering and then plunge diving—form the mainstay of their diet. Placida, Florida, USA. **INSET**: The range of the Osprey.

PAGE 89: These Cooper's Hawk nestlings are only a few days from being able to take their first flight. When fully-grown, the females are larger than the males. This species has short, broad wings with rounded tips and a long tail. They are found in woodlands where they hunt small animals, including birds. New Mexico, USA. **INSET**: The range of the Cooper Hawk.

Year Round
Summer (breeding)
Winter (non-breeding)
Migration

Year Round
Summer (breeding)
Winter (non-breeding)
Migration

RIGHT: The Burrowing Owl is a small, long-legged, migrant species that has brown plumage covered in white spots. It is a ground-dweller that can be found in grassland areas. It is an opportunist that will feed on insects and small animals including rodents, reptiles, amphibians and birds.

LEFT: The Short-Eared Owl is a medium-sized species that lives in grassland and marshy areas. It has a distinctive low-level flight pattern that can help to identify it. It hunts mainly at dusk and dawn, and has a dark beak that it uses to feed on a variety of small mammals. California, USA.

BELOW: The range of the Short-Eared Owl.

Year Round
Summer (breeding)
Winter (non-breeding)
Migration

RIGHT: The Northern Spotted Owl is the largest subspecies of the Spotted Owl, with a wingspan of around 42 inches. It is a nocturnal species and lives in woodland areas, where it feeds on a variety of small animals. It is restricted to small parts of California, where its status is listed as "threatened."

BELOW: The range of the Northern Spotted Owl.

■ Year Round
■ Summer (breeding)
■ Winter (non-breeding)
■ Migration

RIGHT: The American Kestrel is a small, long-tailed hawk with a wingspan of around 21 inches. It has long, slender wings with which it can hover as it searches for insects and various small mammals. It is distributed across most of the United States. Colorado, USA.

RIGHT INSET: The range of the American Kestrel.

Year Round
Summer (breeding)
Winter (non-breeding)
Migration

Ducks, Geese, Swans and Loons

This section includes the ducks, geese, swans and, because of their physical similarity (although they are taxonomically quite different), the loons. The ducks, geese, and swans, of which there are sixty-one North American species, all belong to the family Anatidaeorder in the order Anseriformes. The loons, on the other hand—of which there are five North American species—belong to the family Gaviidae in the order Gaviiformes. All the birds covered here are adapted for an aquatic existence, with water-shedding feathers, webbed feet, and specially shaped bills. As a result, they are often referred to as waterfowl. One or more of these species can be found almost anywhere there is water, from the open sea to lakes, reservoirs, rivers, and streams. They range from the frozen wastes north of the Arctic Circle, all the way south to the equator.

Depending on the classification system used, there are about thirty-seven species of ducks found in North America. These include the Eiders, Mergansers, Goldeneyes, Scoters, Teals, and Whistling-Ducks as well as many others. Some have magnificent plumage; however, in the past this brought nothing but problems for the species concerned. The Wood Duck, for instance, faced extinction in the early 1900s because it was hunted remorselessly for its spectacular feathers. Fortunately, conservation efforts have managed to restore their numbers and even expand their range.

There are six species of geese regularly found in North America—these are the Brant, Canada Goose, Emperor Goose, Greater White-fronted Goose, Ross's Goose, and Snow Goose. The Barnacle Goose, however, is an occasional visitor from Europe. The Brant is adapted to be able to expel salt through special glands—this allows it to eat plants that grow in saltwater, such as eel grass and sea lettuce. The Canada Goose is a well-known bird that can be seen across most of the continent, making itself at home on ponds, fields, and any convenient areas of grass. It is especially noticeable when it makes its way on its annual migrations in large, noisy, "V"-shaped formations. There are several subspecies of Canada Goose, the smallest of which is only the size of a Mallard, and is found in western Alaska. Most geese are herbivores, with various grasses being a common staple.

Three species of swans are found in North America—the Mute Swan, Trumpeter Swan, and Tundra Swan. The Trumpeter Swan is the largest species of waterfowl native to North America, and by some measures (including weight) the continent's largest native bird. The Mute Swan is also a large bird, but it was originally introduced from Europe in small numbers for its ornamental qualities. Its population has since expanded tremendously, and its aggressive behavior and voracious appetite for vegetation has made it extremely unpopular in some areas. Other native aquatic birds have been displaced by the Mute Swan; consequently, they face being wiped out unless something is done. There have been calls for its numbers to be reduced by hunting; however, this is a sensitive issue because the swan is such an emotive bird. The Tundra Swan, which is also known as the Whistling Swan, can be seen in the United States during the winter. When spring comes, they migrate north to breed in the northernmost parts of Canada, and Alaska.

Loons are not related to ducks, even though they look quite similar. They are superbly adapted to life in the water, and are excellent divers; however, they are most unwieldy when they come out onto land. They are found in both fresh and salt water in northern areas, where they are best known for their haunting calls.

Year Round

Summer (breeding)

Winter (non-breeding)

Migration

RIGHT: The Mallard lays its eggs in a shallow depression that is scraped in the ground and then lined with vegetation and down from the mother's breast. After an incubation period of around twenty-five to thirty days, the clutch of between one and thirteen eggs hatches. The ducklings, as seen here, are covered in a fine down.

BELOW: The range of the Mallard.

- ▨ Year Round
- ▨ Summer (breeding)
- ▨ Winter (non-breeding)
- ▨ Migration

FAR RIGHT: The Trumpeter Swan was once hunted extensively for its long feathers, which were considered to make the best quill pens, and by the late 1800s faced extinction. Since then, however, its numbers have recovered significantly, and it is now quite common. Yellowstone National Park, Wyoming, USA.

FAR RIGHT INSET: The range of the Trumpeter Swan.

Year Round

Summer (breeding)

Winter (non-breeding)

Migration

RIGHT: Canada Geese—here seen in flight over the Wapusk National Park, Manitoba, Canada—form into pairs either during migration or while they are over-wintering in preparation for the start of the breeding season.

RIGHT: Canada Geese—here seen in flight over the Wapusk National Park, Manitoba, Canada—form into pairs either during migration or while they are over-wintering in preparation for the start of the breeding season.

LEFT: A flock of Canada Geese in flight. Wapusk National Park, Manitoba, Canada.

RIGHT: Geese head south in the skies over southeastern Arkansas. Stuttgart, Arkansas, USA.

LEFT: Trumpeter Swans do not choose a mate until they are about three or four years old. Most then stay together for life, although a small number will change mates at some stage. Many males will not pair again if they lose their partner. Summit Lake, Kenai Peninsula, Alaska, USA.

RIGHT: The Mute Swan is the most numerous species in the swan family. It is a large bird that may weigh up to 30 lbs. (13.5 kg), and grow to a height of nearly 5 feet (1.5 m). It pairs for life and is known to live for up to thirty-five years. Louisville, Kentucky, USA.

RIGHT INSET: The range of the Mute Swan.

PAGE 104: Canada Geese only eat herbivorous material, with aquatic vegetation, grasses, sedges, grain, and berries being particularly favored. They forage in such large flocks, however, that in recent years they have started to become a pest to farmers in some areas. Reelfoot Lake, Lake County, Tennessee, USA.

PAGE 105: Canada Geese (*Branta canadensis*) usually start to migrate south to warmer climes just as the ground begins to freeze. This pair can be seen on a lake in Seattle, Washington, USA.

Year Round
Summer (breeding)
Winter (non-breeding)
Migration

LEFT: The Emperor Goose is a comparatively small bird that breeds around the Bering Sea, where it can be found on mudflats and tundra along the coasts of northwestern Alaska and Kamchatka, Russia. During the spring it builds a nest on the ground in which three to seven eggs are laid. It overwinters in the Aleutian Islands. Homer, Alaska, USA.

BELOW: The range of the Emperor Goose.

Year Round

Summer (breeding)

Winter (non-breeding)

Migration

RIGHT: The Eider is a large sea duck that can be found across much of the northernmost coastlines of the North American and Eurasian continents. It is perhaps best known for its downy breast feathers that are used by humans as a filling material for bedding and other purposes.

RIGHT INSET: The range of the Eider.

Year Round

Summer (breeding)

Winter (non-breeding)

Migration

RIGHT: The Common Loon—seen here with a chick on its back—is known in Europe as the Great Northern Diver. It is distributed across the northern parts of North America and Europe as well as Greenland and Iceland. Their nests are built on a pile of vegetation close to water, where the female lays two eggs. Kamloops, British Columbia, Canada.

BELOW: The range of the Common Loon.

Year Round

Summer (breeding)

Winter (non-breeding)

Migration

FAR RIGHT: The Arctic Loon can be found in parts of northern Eurasia (where it is known as the Black-throated Diver) and western Alaska. Like the other birds in this family, it specializes in diving to great depths to catch its prey, which consist of various species of fish.

FAR RIGHT INSET: The range of the Arctic Loon.

Year Round
Summer (breeding)
Winter (non-breeding)
Migration

RIGHT: During the breeding season, both the male and female Common Loons share the task of building the nest and feeding their young. They are specialist divers, and will go to depths of 200 feet (60 m) to hunt and catch fish. Little Squam Lake, Ashland, New Hampshire, USA.

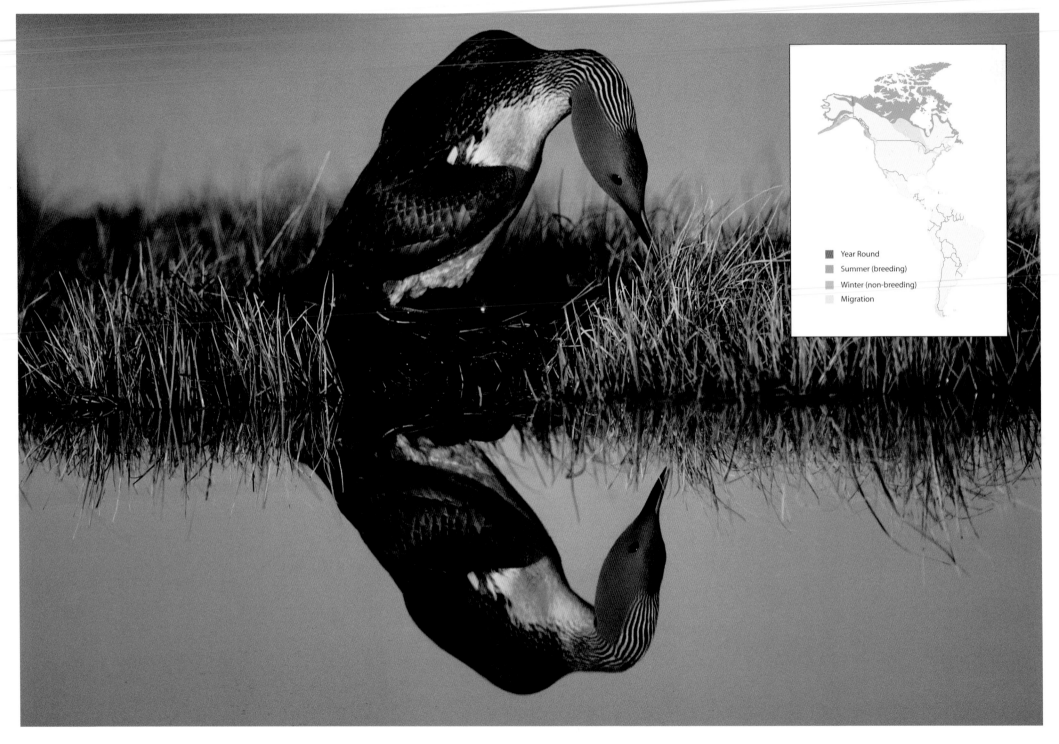

Year Round

Summer (breeding)

Winter (non-breeding)

Migration

LEFT: The Red-throated Loon has a wider range than any other member of its family; it is distributed across the northernmost parts of Eurasia and Canada. It is the smallest of the divers, and hunts at much shallower depths than the others. Arctic National Wildlife Refuge, Alaska, USA.

LEFT INSET: The range of the Red-throated Loon.

RIGHT: The Yellow-billed Loon is the largest member of the diver family, and can be found at sea or on large lakes across the northernmost parts of Eurasia and North America. It hunts for fish such as herring, flounder, and rock cod by diving underwater. Arctic National Wildlife Refuge, Alaska, USA.

BELOW: The range of the The Yellow-billed Loon.

Year Round
Summer (breeding)
Winter (non-breeding)
Migration

FAR LEFT: The Mallard is one of the most commonly seen ducks throughout the North American and Eurasian continents. It forages both on land and in fresh or brackish water for small invertebrates, as well as seeds and aquatic vegetation. It is often seen in parks and gardens where it will happily take food from humans.

LEFT: The Wood Duck is considered by many to be the most beautiful duck in North America. At one time it faced extinction due to the pressures of hunting; however, concerted conservation efforts have managed to turn its fortunes around. San Francisco, California, USA.

BELOW: The range of the Wood Duck.

Year Round

Summer (breeding)

Winter (non-breeding)

Migration

LEFT: The Northern Pintail Duck is distributed across a lot of the northern parts of the North American and Eurasian continents, where it can be found in a wide variety of habitats. Like many other duck species, it feeds on seeds, aquatic vegetation and small invertebrates. Denali National Park and Preserve, Alaska, USA.

BELOW: The range of the Northern Pintail Duck.

Year Round

Summer (breeding)

Winter (non-breeding)

Migration

RIGHT: The Northern Pintail is a medium-sized duck with narrow wings and a pointed tail. It is easily distinguished by its long, slender neck. The males have a reddish head and are marked with strong patterns and have a white chest and a long tail. The females have a dull brown coloration.

LEFT: The American Widgeon is distributed from the northernmost parts of the South American continent, across the United States and all the way up to Alaska. It inhabits shallow freshwater wetland areas, such as ponds, marshes, streams, and rivers, where it forages for aquatic vegetation and small invertebrates.

BELOW: The range of the American Widgeon.

Year Round
Summer (breeding)
Winter (non-breeding)
Migration

RIGHT: The Fulvous Whistling-Duck has one of the widest distributions of any species in its family. It is found across North and South America, as well as parts of Africa and Eurasia. It will often lay its eggs in the nests of other ducks, but in spite of this, stays bonded to its mate for many years. McAllen, Texas, USA.

RIGHT INSET: The range of the Whistling-Duck.

Year Round
Summer (breeding)
Winter (non-breeding)
Migration

RIGHT: The Gadwall is a common duck that can be seen on freshwater ponds and lakes across most of the North American continent, as well as in southern Eurasia and northern Africa. It migrates to the warmer regions during the winter, and then moves north again to breed in the spring. Colorado, USA

RIGHT INSET: The range of the Gadwall.

FAR RIGHT, ABOVE: The Ruddy Duck is one of the smaller members of its family, and is unusual in that it rarely makes any sounds except during its courtship rituals. During the winter it can be found from the coasts of southern Canada down as far as northern Central America and the Caribbean. In the spring it moves further north to breed. Brookgreen Gardens, South Carolina, USA.

FAR RIGHT, ABOVE INSET: The range of the Ruddy Duck.

FAR RIGHT, BELOW: The Red-breasted Merganser is a large diving duck that has a long thin bill. During the breeding season it can be found across Alaska and northern Canada, as well as in some of the north-eastern United States. Elsewhere, it occurs in Greenland, Iceland, and northern Eurasia. Bolsa Chica Wetlands Reserve, California, USA.

■ Year Round
■ Summer (breeding)
■ Winter (non-breeding)
■ Migration

Year Round

Summer (breeding)

Winter (non-breeding)

Migration

Hummingbirds

RIGHT: The Rufous Hummingbird has a wider range than any other hummingbird in North America. It can be seen across all of the contiguous United States and most of Canada during the warmer months. It then flies south as the temperature falls and overwinters in Mexico. Monterey, California, USA.

FAR RIGHT: The Buff-bellied Hummingbird can be found across Mexico and the southern United States. The sexes are very similar, though the male is slightly bigger. They build their nests in low bushes— here an adult is feeding one of its chicks. Raymondville, Texas, USA.

Year Round
Summer (breeding)
Winter (non-breeding)
Migration

ABOVE: There are 16 different breeding species of hummingbird in the United States and space precludes a coverage of all of them. The Ruby-throated Hummingbird by far the most common species that breeds in the eastern half of North America and its range is given as an example.

Hummingbirds are spectacular birds, and often have magnificently colored iridescent feathers. This makes them a popular sight wherever they occur, and they are often encouraged to visit private gardens and public places. The name "hummingbird" comes from the fact that these fascinating little birds beat their wings so fast that it creates a humming sound. The species that are found in North America have a wingbeat that averages a little more than fifty times per second. This unusual method of flying gives them very impressive flight capabilities—they can hover in midair, or even fly backwards. In the wild they feed almost entirely on nectar gathered from flowers, although they will also take sustenance from artificial feeders in parks and backyards. Some species will also feed on tree sap, often from the holes made by sapsuckers. They do not land to feed—instead they hover in front of the food source and insert their long narrow tongues.

The North American continent is home to sixteen different breeding species of hummingbirds—tthe Allen's, Anna's, Black-chinnned, Blue-throated, Broad-billed, Broad-tailed, Buff-bellied, Calliope, Costa's, Green Violet-ear, Lucifer, Magnificent, Ruby-throated, Rufous, Violet-crowned, and White-eared. Other species visit but do not breed. These include the Xantus's Hummingbird, which has been seen in Baja California, the Berylline Hummingbird (southeast Arizona), the Plain-capped Starthroat (southeast Arizona and Mexico), the Green-breasted Mango (south Texas), the Cuban Emerald (south Florida) and the Bahama Woodstar (Florida). Most of the other 322 species are found in South and Central America.

Some people get confused over what is and is not a hummingbird. There are many species of moths, for instance, that fly in exactly the same manner, and for a novice it can be quite hard to distinguish between them. The simplest distinction is size—the bodies of even the smallest North American hummingbirds are nearly four inches in length and more than an inch wide, whereas the biggest moths are much smaller than this.

Humminbirds spend the warmer months building nests and rearing young, then move south during the colder months. In the spring they migrate northwards again, with the males arriving up to three weeks before the females. It is thought that this is to give them time to establish their territories before the breeding season begins. At the end of the season, the males move south first—this may be in order to leave any remaining flowers for the season's new youngsters to feed from. Some species cover incredible distances during their annual migrations—the Ruby-throated Hummingbird, for instance, is believed to fly across the Gulf of Mexico without stopping.

It is thought that most hummingbirds live for between three and four years; however, there are records of some of the larger species living for much longer than this. Although their nests can be raided by a number of different creatures, including snakes and squirrels, adults have very few regular predators. It is likely that the greatest numbers are killed by domestic cats and small birds of prey.

RIGHT: Anna's Hummingbird is one of three species that are resident in the U.S. . It is the most common hummingbird in southern California, and is also the largest species to visit the West Coast.

FAR RIGHT: The Lucifer Hummingbird is found during the warmer months in the southwestern U.S., notably Arizona, New Mexico, and Texas. When winter approaches, it flies to central Mexico until spring returns. The female—as here—is larger than the male, with drab markings.

RIGHT: Hummingbirds normally beat their wings between sixty and eighty times per second. This can increase to about two hundred times per second during the high-speed dives they make during courtship displays. The wing muscles make up about a quarter of body weight.

RIGHT: Costa's Hummingbird has a restricted range, and only breeds in the Sonoran and Mojave deserts of California and Arizona. It the summer it moves to cooler areas of scrub or woodland to escape the worst of the heat. The male, as seen here, has a violet crown. The female has more drab coloration.

RIGHT: The Violet-crowned Hummingbird is primarily a bird of tropical and subtropical regions. As a result, it only visits the more southerly parts of the United States, although it is commonly seen in Mexico. The sexes are very similar, although the male has a brighter coloration and is slightly bigger. El Valle, Panama.

LEFT: The Snowy-bellied Hummingbird is a species of the tropics and is found across much of Central America and the more southerly parts of the North American continent. It is an adaptable bird, being found from sea level up to altitudes of 7,000 feet or more. El Valle, Panama.

RIGHT: The survival of Costa's Hummingbird, like so many others, is under threat from habitat degradation—especially the loss of coastal and Sonoran Desert scrub. Although this species is adapted to feed on nectar from flowers, like many others in this family it will also take small insects when the opportunity arises. USA.

LEFT: The Broad-Billed Hummingbird can be seen across most of the United States and as far north as Ontario, Canada. The sexes are markedly different—this beautifully colored individual is a male. The female is slightly smaller, and has far less resplendent colors, being mostly green and gray. Arizona, USA.

RIGHT: In the United States, there are sixteen species of breeding hummingbirds; however, another six or so vagrant species from Mexico and the Caribbean have also been recorded. Some intrepid hummingbirds—about four or five different kinds—have even made it to Alaska. This is a Broad-billed Hummingbird. Arizona, USA.

LEFT: Hummingbirds have such control over their flight that they are able to hold their heads perfectly still—even when there is a wind blowing. This allows them to feed with great precision. The individual seen here is a Broad-Billed Hummingbird. Arizona, USA.

RIGHT: Hummingbirds normally have a body temperature of around 40°C (104°F). To conserve energy, they lower this by up to 20°C (30°F) at night. In the morning, they must warm up again before they can function properly. Arizona, USA.

PAGE 138: The Ruby-throated Hummingbird needs to eat the equivalent of one to one and a half times its own weight in nectar every day. This is because the muscles it uses to generate its incredibly high wing beat are extremely energy intensive. Here a female is investigating a flower at the same time as a bumblebee. Pennsylvania, USA.

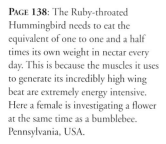

PAGE 139: The throat feathers on the male Anna's Hummingbird display incredible metallic rose-red colors that glisten in the light. The female, in stark contrast, has a white throat with a few red spots. Juveniles of the species have similar markings to the females. Los Osos, California, USA.

ABOVE: Female Anna's Hummingbirds, such as this one sitting on her eggs, lack the iridescent colors of the males. This is partly so that they are more unobtrusive on the nest, and partly because they do not have to attract mates—they do all the choosing. San Luis Obispo, California, USA.

RIGHT: Although this is a Ruby-Throated Hummingbird, it lacks the bright coloration that gave the species its name; this is because it is a female. Only the males have ruby-colored throats. Both sexes are easily attracted to feeders, even those placed close to the windows of occupied rooms. Pennsylvania, USA.

Passerines

More than half of all the kinds of birds in the world are "Passerines," represented by fifty-nine families and more than 5,400 different species. They all belong to the order "Passeriformes" and although they are sometimes referred to as songbirds, a more accurate term is "perching birds." This perching ability results from the fact that passerines have three forward-pointing and one backward-pointing toes—which all lie on the same level and are unwebbed—a unique arrangement among birds. Another general characteristic is that passerines usually lay colored eggs, whereas (with few exceptions), most other birds' eggs are white. The group covers an incredible range of different types, from wrens to birds of paradise, and from mockingbirds to wagtails. The order is split into three further groups—these are the suborders Tyranni, Passeri (Corvida), and Passeri (Passerida). All of the Passerines are land birds, and many are well known to most people—they include such commonly seen examples as blackbirds, chickadees, crows, and sparrows.

Although the name "Passerine" means "sparrow-shaped," many of the group's members do not look like at all sparrow-like. The largest North American species is the Common Raven, which grows to between 22 and 27 inches in length, and has a wingspan of around 50 inches—most of the rest of the group are quite small though. Even though the Ruby-crowned Kinglet is the smallest, it lays the heaviest clutch of eggs, relative to its size. In spite of the fact that each egg only weighs 0.65g (0.02 oz), the combined weight of up to twelve eggs can equal the body mass of the mother bird.

It is thought that the perching birds are the most highly evolved of all birds, and are also considered by many scientists to be the most intelligent. A large number of them have very well-developed and complex vocalizations, or calls—hence the reason why they are also known as songbirds. When the breeding season begins, the males of many species take up residence in a particular area, and attempt to stake a claim to it using territorial "songs." While these may simply sound like beautiful tunes to us, they are of great importance to the birds concerned. Those that transgress a given territory may well end up in an aggressive battle with the previous owner, and will sometimes even fight to the death.

Perching birds have been successful in all the various terrestrial habitats, from the frozen wastes of the north to the tropics of the equatorial regions. Some, such as the swallow, specialize in catching food—in this case flying insects—on the wing. Others hunt for small creatures hiding in tree bark or flowers, or may feed exclusively on plant seeds. Many migrate with the seasons to take advantage of good weather conditions and the availability of food. Consequently, they move north in the spring, and then return south again as winter approaches. The swallows and martins are one of the more instantly recognizable examples of species undertaking this seasonal movement.

Year Round

Summer (breeding)

Winter (non-breeding)

Migration

LEFT: Many people consider the male Painted Bunting to be the most beautiful bird in North America. Its incredible coloration is so distinctive that it is almost impossible to mistake it for anything else. Unsurprisingly, this makes it very popular as a cage bird, and while this is illegal in the U.S. and Canada, trapping still occurs in Mexico and Central America. Roma, Texas, USA.

LEFT INSET: The range of the Painted Bunting.

RIGHT: The Lark Sparrow is found in southern Canada, a large part of the U.S., and in northern Mexico. It is one of the larger members of its family and its diet is mostly composed of seeds. However, it will also capture insects, especially grasshoppers during the breeding season. Edinburg, Texas, USA.

RIGHT INSET: The range of the Lark Sparrow.

Year Round
Summer (breeding)
Winter (non-breeding)
Migration

RIGHT: The Long-billed Thrasher only occurs in southern Texas and eastern Mexico. It inhabits areas that are primarily composed of dense, scrubby thickets, where it forages on the ground for small invertebrates such as insects, spiders, and snails. It will also eat berries when it finds them. Roma, Texas, USA.

BELOW: The range of the Long-billed Thrasher.

Year Round

Summer (breeding)

Winter (non-breeding)

Migration

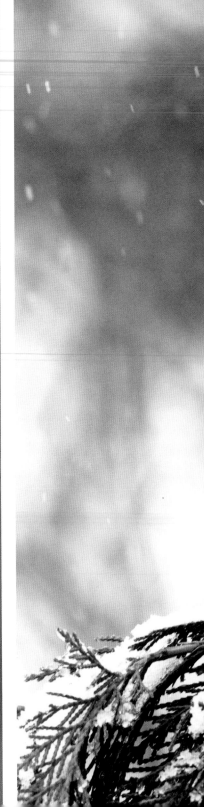

LEFT: The Northern Cardinal can be found from Canada southwards as far as Guatemala. It is one of the few bird species that has really benefited from the changes made to the environment by mankind—its population has increased significantly over the last 200 years. McLeansville, North Carolina, USA.

BELOW: The range of the Northern Cardinal.

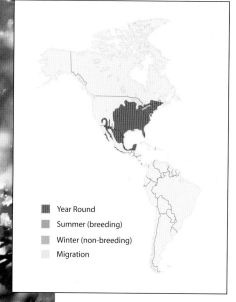

Year Round

Summer (breeding)

Winter (non-breeding)

Migration

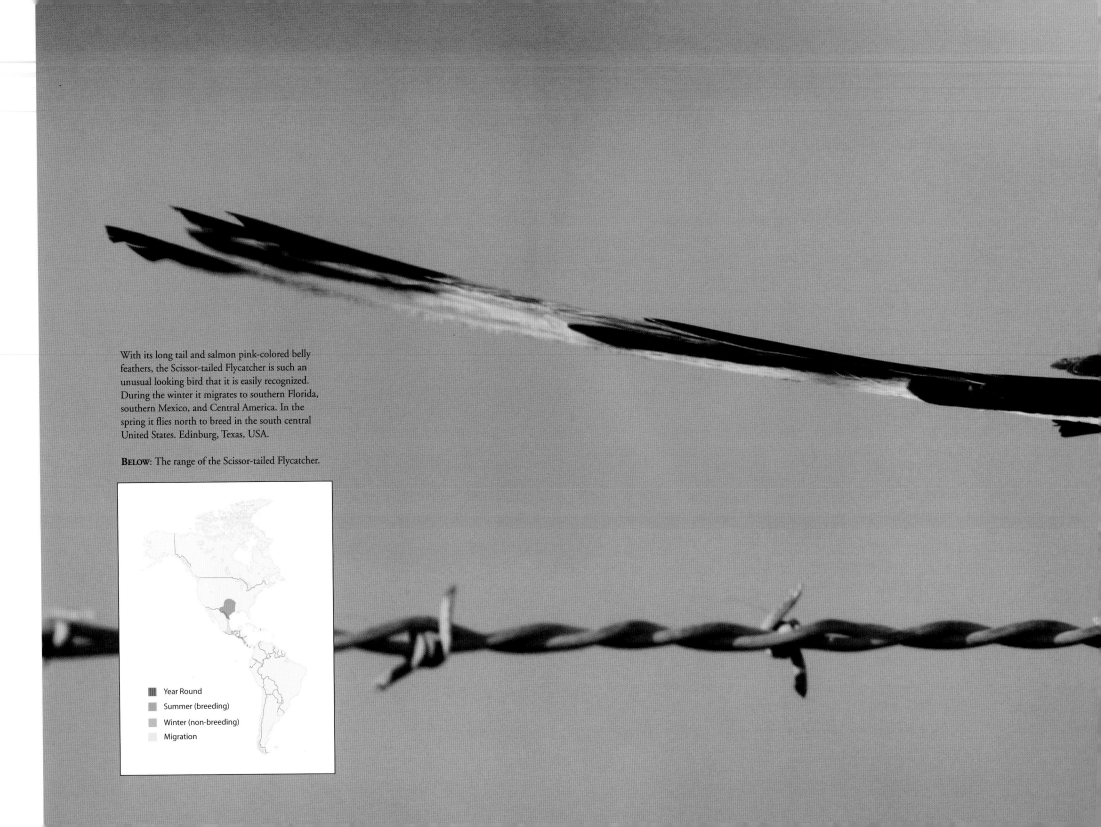

With its long tail and salmon pink-colored belly feathers, the Scissor-tailed Flycatcher is such an unusual looking bird that it is easily recognized. During the winter it migrates to southern Florida, southern Mexico, and Central America. In the spring it flies north to breed in the south central United States. Edinburg, Texas, USA.

BELOW: The range of the Scissor-tailed Flycatcher.

■ Year Round
■ Summer (breeding)
■ Winter (non-breeding)
■ Migration

BELOW: The range of the Mountain Bluebird.

Year Round

Summer (breeding)

Winter (non-breeding)

Migration

RIGHT: While the Bronzed Cowbird can be seen in the southern border states and Louisiana, it is primarily a Central American species. It does not build a nest of its own, but instead lays its eggs in the nests of other species. It forages for food on open ground, where it will eat various seeds and small invertebrates. Roma, Texas, USA.

RIGHT INSET: The range of the Bronzed Cowbird.

Year Round
Summer (breeding)
Winter (non-breeding)
Migration

Year Round
Summer (breeding)
Winter (non-breeding)
Migration

FAR LEFT: The American Robin is a well-loved bird that is familiar to most inhabitants of North America. In the winter they assemble in enormous flocks made up of several hundred thousand individuals. These gather together in woodlands from Oregon to Mexico, before breaking up again at the start of the breeding season.

FAR LEFT INSET: The range of the American Robin.

LEFT: The Pine Warbler, as its name would suggest, is a bird of pine woodlands. It is only found in the eastern part of North America, from southeastern Manitoba to Florida. It overwinters in the southeastern United States; most then fly farther north to breed. McLeansville, North Carolina, USA.

BELOW: The range of the Pine Warbler.

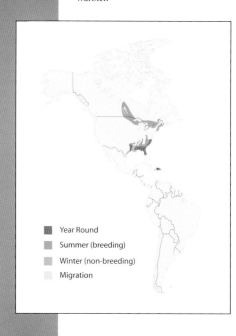

Year Round

Summer (breeding)

Winter (non-breeding)

Migration

Year Round

Summer (breeding)

Winter (non-breeding)

Migration

LEFT: The White-eyed Vireo is a small songbird that fossil evidence shows has lived in North America for at least 400,000 years. It overwinters in the southern United States and down into northern Central America and the Caribbean. With the arrival of spring it flies north as far as southern Ontario to breed. Collier County, Florida, USA.

LEFT INSET: The range of the White-eyed Vireo.

RIGHT: The Grey-crowned Rosy Finch is found in the Pacific Northwest in extreme alpine environments. It usually breeds near snowfields, glaciers, or cliffs. It forages for small creatures and seeds in trees and on the ground, but will also catch flying insects if the opportunity arises. Homer, Alaska, USA.

BELOW: The range of the Grey-crowned Rosy Finch.

Year Round
Summer (breeding)
Winter (non-breeding)
Migration

PAGE 154: The White-throated Sparrow—of which there are two color forms–is distributed from northern Mexico across most of the U.S. from the Rockies east, and north into Canada. It overwinters in the southern reaches of this region, and then migrates north in the spring to breed in dense woodlands. McLeansville, North Carolina, USA.

BELOW: The range of the White-throated Sparrow.

- Year Round
- Summer (breeding)
- Winter (non-breeding)
- Migration

RIGHT: The Grey-crowned Rosy Finch is found in the Pacific Northwest in extreme alpine environments. It usually breeds near snowfields, glaciers, or cliffs. It forages for small creatures and seeds in trees and on the ground, but will also catch flying insects if the opportunity arises. Homer, Alaska, USA.

LEFT: Eastern Bluebirds—this is a male—are very popular sights in gardens and public spaces. In some places they are a traditional symbol of happiness, however, they are often preyed upon by racoons and domestic cats. McLeansville, North Carolina, USA.

BELOW: The range of the Eastern Bluebird.

Year Round
Summer (breeding)
Winter (non-breeding)
Migration

RIGHT: The Hooded Oriole is named after the black facial markings found in the male of the species. It is found in the southwestern United States, and can often be seen hanging upside down as it forages for insects, spiders, nectar, and fruit. Arizona, USA.

RIGHT INSET: The range of the Hooded Oriole.

Year Round
Summer (breeding)
Winter (non-breeding)
Migration

RIGHT: Although the female Northern Cardinal has a similar overall shape to that of the male, its plumage has a very different coloration. While the black facemask is still present, the male's vivid reds are replaced by a gray-brown color with a few traces of red here and there. McLeansville, North Carolina, USA.

RIGHT: The Tufted Titmouse is common in deciduous forest areas as well as swamps and suburban areas ranging from southern Ontario to the Gulf Coast. It feeds on small insects and seeds, usually by hanging upside-down; it often does this in the company of birds of other species. McLeansville, North Carolina, USA.

BELOW: The range of the Tufted Titmouse.

Year Round

Summer (breeding)

Winter (non-breeding)

Migration

Left: The Blue Jay is a large songbird that is a frequent visitor to bird feeders, where its distinctive plumage makes it easy to identify. It will eat a wide variety of different foodstuffs, including nuts, fruits, seeds, and even small vertebrates such as frogs and lizards. McLeansville, North Carolina, USA.

Below: The range of the Blue Jay.

Year Round
Summer (breeding)
Winter (non-breeding)
Migration

Right: The Eastern Bluebird is a well known visitor to many gardens and parks and can be found in open habitat from Canada in the north to Central America in the south. It feeds on small invertebrates, fruits, and berries. Here an adult female can be seen in the process of feeding her chick. McLeansville, North Carolina, USA.

Year Round
Summer (breeding)
Winter (non-breeding)
Migration

Left: The Common Grackle has distinctive iridescent plumage that shimmers with various wonderful hues of blue, green, purple, and bronze. This coloration, together with its characteristic long tail, makes it an easy species to recognize. It is an extreme opportunist, taking advantage of almost any chance to feed. McLeansville, North Carolina, USA.

Left inset: The range of the Common Grackle.

Right: The Pyrrhuloxia is a songbird that can be found across the southwestern United States and Mexico. It inhabits dry scrubland, open grasslands, and woods along the edges of rivers and streams, foraging for seeds, fruits, and insects, although it will readily visit feeders. Arizona, USA.

Below: The range of the Pyrrhuloxia.

Year Round
Summer (breeding)
Winter (non-breeding)
Migration

RIGHT: The Carolina Chickadee's range is restricted to the southeastern United States, where it can be found in deciduous and mixed woodlands, as well as in wetlands and parks. Typically it nests in holes in trees, but will also happily use nest boxes; it lays a clutch of between three and ten eggs.

BELOW: The range of the Carolina Chickadee.

Year Round

Summer (breeding)

Winter (non-breeding)

Migration

FAR RIGHT: The Red-breasted Nuthatch can be found in coniferous and mixed forests from southern Alaska down to the Gulf Coast. As with the other nuthatch species, it feeds by searching tree bark for small invertebrates such as insects and spiders, but also eats conifer seeds. Portland, Oregon, USA.

FAR RIGHT INSET: The range of the Red-breasted Nuthatch.

Year Round

Summer (breeding)

Winter (non-breeding)

Migration

LEFT: The White-breasted Nuthatch inhabits deciduous forests across North America, from southern Canada to southern Mexico. It can often be seen scouring tree trunks for insects — usually traveling in a head-downwards position—or searching branches for nuts and seeds. It will also visit feeders. McLeansville, North Carolina, USA.

BELOW: The range of the White-breasted Nuthatch.

Year Round
Summer (breeding)
Winter (non-breeding)
Migration

RIGHT: During the winter, the Brown Thrasher is found from southern Missouri southeast to southern Florida. When spring arrives, it flies north as far as southern Canada to breed, where it builds its nests in dense scrub and hedgerows. It feeds on small invertebrates as well as fruits, berries, and nuts. McLeansville, North Carolina, USA.

RIGHT INSET: The range of the Brown Thrasher.

Year Round

Summer (breeding)

Winter (non-breeding)

Migration

LEFT: The Chestnut-backed Chickadee, which is the smallest of its family, is only found along the Pacific coast in dense woodland. Its range extends from southern Alaska and down to southern California. Although it usually feeds high in trees, it will readily visit bird feeders. Portland, Oregon, USA.

BELOW: The range of the Chestnut-backed Chickadee.

Year Round

Summer (breeding)

Winter (non-breeding)

Migration

RIGHT: The Song Sparrow is a common bird that is aptly named—its songs can be heard throughout the warmer months of the year across most of North America, from Mexico to Alaska. It lives in open, shrubby areas including gardens, where it eats a variety of different seeds, fruits and invertebrates.

RIGHT INSET: The range of the Song Sparrow.

Year Round

Summer (breeding)

Winter (non-breeding)

Migration

ABOVE AND RIGHT: The male Northern Cardinal has unmistakable red plumage and a large red crest on its head. It is a popular bird and readily visits feeders during the winter, especially those stocked with sunflower seeds, although its usual diet consists of a mixture of seeds, fruits, berries, and insects. Big Cypress Swamp, Florida, USA.

FAR RIGHT: The nest of the American Robin is usually located among the branches of a low tree or shrub. It is made up of a mass of interwoven grass and twigs that are then bound together with mud and lined with dry grass. The typical clutch is made up of three to four eggs.

Seabirds

RIGHT: Pelicans can often be seen in large numbers basking in the sun along many of the coasts of North America. This allows them to make sure that their feathers are completely clean and dry before they set out for another bout of fishing.

There are many different ways to define what a seabird is—here, we are including birds that spend the majority of their lives on oceans or seas. Several kinds that are on the edges of this definition have been assigned to other chapters. These include the loons, which are types of ducks, and birds of prey such as the Osprey and the Bald Eagle, both of which include individuals that spend a vast amount of time feeding from the sea. Birds that are covered here include the auks, cormorants, gannets, gulls, pelicans, skimmers, skuas, and terns. Many, such as the pelican, are as equally at home on bodies of freshwater as they are at sea, and so are hard to categorize.

Although many seabirds live far out at sea, they all have to return to land to breed. In most species both parents share the job of raising the nestlings. This is often an absolute necessity, because unguarded nests are usually quickly raided by gulls or other predatory birds who will take and eat eggs or chicks without hesitation. Once the survivors have fledged, the juveniles of some species head out to sea and may not see land again for up to two years. After this time they are mature enough to breed, and so return to the shore to find a mate and build a nest.

During the summer months, the waters of the Arctic and sub-Arctic teem with life, and so provide a bountiful supply of food for hungry seabirds. Consequently, enormous numbers move north every spring—along the way, the coastline becomes swamped with hundreds of thousands of migrating birds. In the space of a few weeks, the cliffs of places like Newfoundland and Labrador are turned into some of the largest seabird colonies in the world. These are noisy places; sometimes they are called "bazaars," after the noise and chaos found in Middle Eastern marketplaces. Typically, many different species—gannets, kittiwakes, razorbills, and so on—will nest alongside each other. Among them will be small numbers of predators or opportunists such as ravens, crows, and aggressive gulls who will feed their young by stealing easy meals from unguarded nests.

The birds from these vast colonies often team up into dense flocks to feed from the large schools of fish that can often be found in northern waters. Each species has its own method of hunting—some dive after their prey, whereas others swim or simply plunge into the water to find a meal. Once the brief northern summer is over, however, they have to move south again as the increasingly cold weather and shorter days signal the return of winter. Many head for subtropical regions, but some travel a lot farther. The Arctic Tern, for instance, migrates from North America across to the coast of Africa, and then travels south all the way to Antarctica. In doing so, they cover more than 20,000 miles per year.

Unfortunately, modern fishing practices have reduced the level of fish stocks to such an extent that many seabird species have declined dramatically. Others, such as members of the auk family, are very vulnerable to oil pollution, and vast numbers can be killed by a single spill. Efforts are being made to conserve these beautiful birds, but there is still a long way to go, especially if global warming continues to accelerate.

Year Round

Summer (breeding)

Winter (non-breeding)

Migration

LEFT: The Northern Gannet is a large sea bird that hunts for fish by diving. It does this by closing its wings at a height of about 40 meters (130 feet) and plunging into the water at an incredible speed. This allows it to reach depths of up to 22 meters (72 feet). It is found on the Gulf of St. Lawrence, Québec, and along the coast of Newfoundland as well as in Northern Europe.

LEFT INSET: The range of the Northern Gannet.

RIGHT: The Brown Pelican is a large bird, with a wingspan that reaches around 200 cm (79 inches). It is adept at soaring for long periods in the search for schools of fish—before closing its wings and plunging into the water after them. La Jolla Reefs, San Diego Bay, California, USA.

BELOW: The range of the Brown Pelican.

- Year Round
- Summer (breeding)
- Winter (non-breeding)
- Migration

FAR LEFT: Pelicans have a slow lumbering flight when compared to other, similarly sized birds, such as the Bald Eagle. This is mainly because they catch their prey in the water, and so do not need to waste energy by flying fast. Key West, Florida, USA.

LEFT: Since Brown Pelicans (*Pelecanus occidentalis*) have few natural predators and are rarely disturbed by humans, they can often be seen at close quarters. Cabo San Lucas, Mexico.

177

RIGHT: Brown Pelicans are found along both the coasts of the United States—from California in the west and Maryland in the east—down to South America. It catches fish by plunge-diving and trapping them in its huge pouch before eating them. Baja California, Mexico.

FAR RIGHT: The Black Skimmer is unique among North American birds in that the lower half of its bill is longer than the top half. This allows it to catch fish by flying above water with the lower part under the surface—any fish it encounters are then snapped up and eaten. Florida, USA.

FAR RIGHT INSET: The range of the Black Skimmer.

PAGE 180: These four Pelicans, silhouetted against the vivid red backdrop of a setting sun, are returning to their regular roosting site before nightfall.

PAGE 181: Three seagulls in flight at sunset. Carolina Beach, Wilmington, North Carolina, USA.

Year Round

Summer (breeding)

Winter (non-breeding)

Migration

LEFT: While many species of birds have declined as the direct consequence of human activity, the populations of many species of seagulls have boomed. California, USA.

LEFT: Seagulls like to roost on cliff faces and other rocky places where they have a good view of the landscape and are out of the way of predators. La Jolla Reefs, San Diego Bay, California, USA.

BELOW: The range of the Herring Gull, the most widespread North American gull.

Year Round

Summer (breeding)

Winter (non-breeding)

Migration

LEFT: Terns are gregarious creatures that often gather in flocks that are made up of enormous numbers of birds. Fort DeSoto Park, Florida, USA.

BELOW: The range of the Tern.

Year Round
Summer (breeding)
Winter (non-breeding)
Migration

RIGHT: The Arctic Tern is remarkable for the incredible migrations it undertakes every year. It breeds in the Arctic, but at the end of the season it flies all the way to Antarctica to overwinter—a round-trip of around 40,000 km (25,000 miles), which is a longer journey than that made by any other bird. Wapusk National Park, Manitoba, Canada.

RIGHT INSET: The range of the Arctic Tern.

Year Round

Summer (breeding)

Winter (non-breeding)

Migration

LEFT: The Black Tern can be found in North and South America, as well as Africa and Eurasia. It inhabits freshwater marshes, where it hunts for fish and small invertebrates and is usually seen in flocks that can number many thousands of birds. Kamloops, British Columbia, Canada.

RIGHT: The Arctic Tern is a long-lived bird, considering its size. Individuals have been known to reach the age of thirty-four; however, it does not reach maturity until it is three to four years old. Its nest is made either by scraping a hollow on open ground, or on a low pile of vegetation. Nome, Alaska, USA.

LEFT: The Common Tern is the most widespread member of its family, being found on every continent except Antarctica. It can often be seen hovering and plunge-diving for small fish in lakes and rivers or the sea. It will also capture small invertebrates when the opportunity arises.

RIGHT: The Laughing Gull can be found all the way from Maine down the coasts of North and Central America and into South America. It will eat more or less anything that it can find, including small aquatic and terrestrial invertebrates, fish, flying insects, fruit, berries, and, of course, garbage.

BELOW: The range of the Laughing Gull.

Year Round
Summer (breeding)
Winter (non-breeding)
Migration

LEFT: The shoreline can be a good source of food for a hungry sea bird. The tide line is often rich with washed-up debris, including garbage discarded by humans and all types of dead sea life. Below the sand, there are also teeming hordes of small invertebrates. Manhattan Beach Pier, California, USA.

PAGE 192–193: Where freshwater rivers and streams discharge into the sea, they often provide an increase in the local nutrient supply—this results in increased numbers of small organisms. Consequently, many sea birds can be seen congregating there to feed. Pistol River State Park, Oregon, USA.

Year Round

Summer (breeding)

Winter (non-breeding)

Migration

ABOVE AND RIGHT: Cormorants are expert fish-catchers. They make prolonged dives, during which time they find, chase, and capture their prey. In the Far East, it used to be common for fishermen to tie lengths of thin rope to captive birds and then use them to catch fish. Everglades National Park, Florida, USA.

LEFT: There are six types of cormorants native to North America. The most numerous and widespread is the Double-crested Cormorant, whose range is shown here.

FAR RIGHT: The Atlantic Puffin is an unmistakable sea bird that nests in large colonies along the coasts of small islands on both the American and European sides of the North Atlantic Ocean. It uses its large bill to catch and hold small fish until it either eats them or delivers them to its young.

INSET: The range of the Atlantic Puffin.

Year Round

Summer (breeding)

Winter (non-breeding)

Migration

Shorebirds

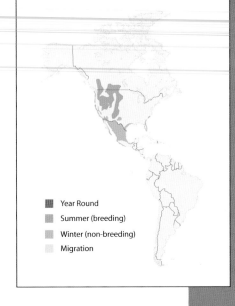

Year Round

Summer (breeding)

Winter (non-breeding)

Migration

In North America forty-nine species of shorebirds are commonly seen—these include avocets, oystercatchers, phalaropes, plovers, sandpipers, snipes, stilts, and turnstones. They can be seen on beaches as well as along estuaries and on marshes and mudflats. Most have relatively small bodies and long, thin legs; however, they are distinct from seabirds in that they do not swim. One simple method to distinguish between the two categories is that whereas seabirds have webbed feet, shorebirds do not.

Because the shoreline teems with life, it is a very rich place for birds to forage. Consequently, the various species tend to specialize in specific feeding methods. Many have evolved distinctively shaped bills—the American Avocet, for instance, has a long slender bill that curves gracefully upwards. It uses its bill to catch small aquatic invertebrates in shallow water and soft mud by sweeping its head from side to side in a sifting manner. In contrast, while curlews (of which there are two species in North America) are very similar birds that feed on a similar diet, their bills curve downwards. They use their bills in a probing action, seeking out small crabs and other similar creatures. Although the American Avocet's upswept bill is a very efficient shape for gathering food along the shoreline, it is far less suitable elsewhere. This means that it has to live near water all its life, including during the breeding season. Curlews, however, can feed on dry or wet ground, and so are able to fly to highland areas to raise their young, away from the majority of predators. Other birds, such as plovers use their keen eyesight to find food, and then eat it using short bills. These differences in habit mean that many kinds of birds can feed harmoniously alongside each other because they are not competing with each other. Consequently, one can often see a wide variety of different shorebirds densely packed together on mudflats or beaches.

Many shorebirds migrate to find the best feeding or breeding areas. Significant numbers fly to the sub-Arctic and Arctic tundra before the breeding season starts, and then fly south to overwinter in warmer climes before winter returns. Some of these travel as far as South America, although the majority remain in Central America, the Caribbean, and the southern United States. These annual migrations involve huge numbers, and as a result favored resting spots along the way can often be swamped by tens of thousands of tired and hungry birds. Some of these migratory species fly staggering distances without stopping. The Bristle-thighed Curlew, for instance, is capable of covering 1,200 to 3,000 miles between stops. While the Red Knot stops more often, it travels much farther, flying from the Arctic Circle in the north to destinations as far south as Tierra del Fuego, on the furthest tip of South America.

Nonmigratory shorebird species often breed in wetland areas, although some such as Oystercatchers nest on sandy beaches, and Common Snipe nest in meadows and highland areas. Several shorebird species such as the Eskimo Curlew, Piping Plover, and Snowy Plover are endangered, and many others are showing a general population decline. The main causes are loss of wetland or breeding habitats and environmental pollution; however, their plight is not helped by predation from seagulls, crows, foxes, and other mammals.

RIGHT: The Sanderling—seen here in its winter plumage—is one of the most widely distributed shorebirds, being found on almost every shoreline in the world (with the exception of Antarctica). They breed in the extreme north of the North American and Eurasian continents. Fort DeSoto Park, Florida, USA.

BELOW: The range of the Sanderling.

Year Round

Summer (breeding)

Winter (non-breeding)

Migration

FAR RIGHT: During the winter, the Least Sandpiper, the smallest shorebird in the world, can be found on damp ground anywhere between Oregon and central South America. When spring arrives, it flies north to breed on the wet tundra of Alaska and northern Canada. Fort DeSoto Park, Florida, USA.

FAR RIGHT INSET: The range of the Least Sandpiper.

RIGHT: The Marbled Godwit has a long bill with a slight upwards curve—this allows it to probe the ground for small invertebrates and crustaceans. It breeds on marshland and other wet areas and then overwinters on both the Pacific and Atlantic coasts from the southern U.S. to Central America. Fort DeSoto Park, Florida, USA.

BELOW: The range of the Marbled Godwit.

- Year Round
- Summer (breeding)
- Winter (non-breeding)
- Migration

FAR RIGHT: The Western Sandpiper, seen here in its breeding plumage, migrates in huge flocks to its summer grounds in western Alaska and eastern Siberia. It nests on coastal sedge-dwarf tundra, and then flies south to overwinter on various wetland habitats anywhere between the Pacific Coast and central South America. Cordova, Alaska, USA.

FAR RIGHT INSET: The range of the Western Sandpiper.

Year Round

Summer (breeding)

Winter (non-breeding)

Migration

Year Round
Summer (breeding)
Winter (non-breeding)
Migration

FAR LEFT: The American Golden-Plover is a large shorebird that can be seen on various kinds of open ground, from mudflats to grasslands. It breeds in Canada, Alaska, and Siberia and migrates to central and southern South America to overwinter. Nome, Alaska, USA.

FAR LEFT INSET: The range of the American Golden-Plover.

LEFT: The Rock Sandpiper is a variable bird, with many distinct populations. It breeds on damp tundra along the coasts of western Alaska and the easternmost parts of Siberia. As winter approaches, it flies south—as far as northern California for the American populations, and Japan for the Russian ones. Homer, Alaska, USA.

BELOW: The range of the Rock Sandpiper.

Year Round

Summer (breeding)

Winter (non-breeding)

Migration

RIGHT: With its dramatically upturned bill and eye-catching plumage, the American Avocet is easily identified. It feeds by sweeping its bill from side to side through shallow water, in the process filtering out any small creatures living there. Salton Sea National Wildlife Refuge, California, USA.

BELOW: The range of the American Avocet.

Year Round
Summer (breeding)
Winter (non-breeding)
Migration

FAR RIGHT: The Piping Plover is a small bird that occurs in several distinct populations, all of which are either considered endangered or threatened. During the winter it inhabits wetlands, where it hunts for insects and aquatic invertebrates. In the breeding season, it migrates to various grounds, including the northern Great Plains, the Great Lakes, and parts of the northern Atlantic Coast. Gray's Beach, Cape Cod, Massachusetts, USA.

FAR RIGHT INSET: The range of the Piping Plover.

Year Round

Summer (breeding)

Winter (non-breeding)

Migration

Year Round

Summer (breeding)

Winter (non-breeding)

Migration

LEFT: The Clapper Rail is a medium-sized shorebird that is very common on saltwater marshes and in mangrove swamps. It feeds on a variety of different foodstuffs, including fish, crustaceans, insects, and seeds. It is found along both the Atlantic and Pacific coasts from Massachusetts and California to South America. San Francisco, California, USA.

LEFT INSET: The range of the Clapper Rail.

LEFT: The Black-necked Stilt is easily recognized because of its long, red legs—only the flamingo has longer legs in relation to its body size. It can be seen in shallow wetland areas where it forages for small invertebrates by wading and swimming. San Francisco, California, USA.

BELOW: The range of the Black-necked Stilt.

■ Year Round
■ Summer (breeding)
■ Winter (non-breeding)
■ Migration

PAGE 208: During the breeding season, the American Avocet can be very aggressive toward potential predators and will physically attack birds of prey if they get too close to the nest. Once the eggs have hatched, the chicks are able to walk, swim, and dive within one day. San Francisco, California, USA.

PAGE 209: There are two subspecies of Clapper Rail—one on the east coast, and the other on the west coast. The eastern form is very common; however, western populations are considered endangered. Although most are resident throughout the year, those in the northernmost areas migrate south to overwinter. California, USA.

LEFT: The Long-Billed Curlew's beak is adapted so that it can find and capture small creatures under the surface of water. In inland areas, these are typically worms and insect larvae, whereas in coastal habitats they are more likely to be marine organisms such as small crustaceans. Fort De Soto, Florida, USA.

RIGHT: The Dunlin is a very common bird that is found along the northern coasts of both the North American and Eurasian continents. It stands about 9 inches tall, and has a long bill that it uses to probe for small invertebrates in mud and soft soil on mudflats and other wetlands. Fort De Soto Park, Florida, USA.

BELOW: The range of the Dunlin.

Year Round

Summer (breeding)

Winter (non-breeding)

Migration

Year Round

Summer (breeding)

Winter (non-breeding)

Migration

FAR LEFT: The Ruddy Turnstone is a small shorebird that can be seen on mudflats and beaches. Its characteristic behavior is to dart about eating small invertebrates, carrion, and garbage under stones and in seaweed or any washed-up debris. Fort DeSoto County Park, Florida, USA.

FAR LEFT INSET: The range of the Ruddy Turnstone.

LEFT: The Greater Yellowlegs is a long-legged shorebird that is common in wetland areas from southern Alaska in the west and Newfoundland in the east to the southernmost tip of South America. It feeds in shallow water in two main ways: by sight, and by sweeping its bill from side-to-side and sifting out any prey it encounters. Fort De Soto County Park, Florida, USA.

BELOW: The range of the Greater Yellowlegs.

Year Round

Summer (breeding)

Winter (non-breeding)

Migration

LEFT: The American Oystercatcher is easily identified by its black-and-white plumage and bright red bill. It can be seen along beaches and estuaries in the warmer regions of both the Atlantic and Pacific coasts of North and South America. Fort De Soto Park, Florida, USA.

BELOW: The range of the Oystercatcher.

Year Round
Summer (breeding)
Winter (non-breeding)
Migration

RIGHT: The Red Knot migrates over enormous distances, traveling to and from its breeding grounds in northern Alaska and Canada to the southernmost tip of South America every year. These lovely birds congregate together in massive flocks to make the extensive journey. Fort De Soto Park, Florida, USA.

RIGHT INSET: The range of the Red Knot.

Year Round
Summer (breeding)
Winter (non-breeding)
Migration

Waders and Cranes

RIGHT: Flamingos get their magnificent red or pink coloration from chemical pigments called carotenoids that they absorb when eating small, red-hued shrimp. The pigments then accumulate in the feathers—the degree of coloration is directly linked to the amount of pigment in their food. If they stop eating enough shrimp, their feathers turn pale. Rio Lagartos, Yucatan, Mexico.

RIGHT INSET: The range of the Flamingo.

Year Round Habitat

- American Flamingo
- Andean Flamingo
- James's Flamingo
- Chilean Flamingo

This section covers the waders and cranes; however, because there are several different definitions of exactly what constitutes a wader, it is worth stating that here the group is considered to include the various long-legged species of birds that feed predominantly in water.

There are only two species of crane found in North America: The Sandhill Crane, which is the most numerous of its kind in the world, and the Whooping Crane, which in stark contrast. is the rarest. Both belong to the order Gruiformes, in the family Gruidae, and both have been the subject of significant conservation efforts. Much of the work has focused on restoring previously lost wetland habitats, and a critical part of this has been the development of sustainable land management practices.

There are six different subspecies of Sandhill Crane, with the smallest being the Lesser Sandhill Crane, which stands at only 3.5 feet tall. It breeds in the extreme north, above the Arctic Circle. The largest is the Greater Sandhill Crane, which lives in more temperate areas, grows up to 5 feet tall, and can weigh up to 14 pounds—twice the weight of the Lesser Sandhill Crane. The other subspecies are the Canadian, Mississippi, Cuban, and Florida Cranes.

The population of wild Whooping Cranes fell so low that captive breeding programs were started. Reintroduction schemes have now seen the return of these beautiful birds to several wild places, and at long last their numbers are once again on the increase.

The Greater Flamingo has a debatable status in the United States—most sightings are made in Florida, and although some individuals are known to have flown north from Central America, most of the birds seen there are probably escapees from zoos or private collections. Flamingos do occur naturally in Mexico, though, and so are counted as a true North American species. They feed by filtering small aquatic crustaceans and marine algae from water by bending their long necks until their heads are upside-down. In this position, the beak ably removes edible items from the mud and silt. Their incredible coloration is due to red pigments that are obtained from the food they eat— young flamingos have white feathers until they have eaten sufficient pigmented foods to take on the red hues of the adults.

The other birds in this section all belong to the order Ciconiiformes. They are divided into three families. These are the Ardeidae, the bitterns, egrets, and herons; the Threskiornithidae, the ibises and spoonbills; and the Ciconiidae, the storks. All the birds in this group are primarily wetland species, and feed on small animals, such as frogs, fish, and insects. Some nest in colonies built at the tops of trees, whereas others, like the bittern, nest in reed beds. The Great Blue Heron is a commonly seen example, and is distributed across much of Central and Northern America, more or less wherever there is water in which it can hunt. Like most of the others in the order, it uses its sharp beak to spear its prey, before engulfing it whole.

LEFT: Of the six different species of flamingos, the spectacularly colored Greater Flamingo (*Phoenicopterus ruber*) has the widest distribution, occurring across large parts of the tropical and subtropical areas of the world. It feeds on crustaceans, plankton, and algae in shallow fresh and marine waters. Celestun National Wildlife Refuge, Yucatan, Mexico.

ABOVE: The Great Egret is a stalking hunter; as seen here, it creeps slowly through shallow water towards its intended victim and then lunges forward, using its sharp bill as a spear-like weapon. It can be seen doing this across a variety of wetlands and in ponds, lakes, and rivers. Los Angeles, California, USA.

Left: The Sandhill Crane (*Grus canadensis*) has an ungainly, but effective flight. In spite of the powerful downbeat of its wings, it still manages to keep its head level. Creamers's Field, Fairbanks, Alaska, USA.

Below: The range of the Sandhill Crane.

Year Round

Summer (breeding)

Winter (non-breeding)

Migration

Right: The diet of the Sandhill Crane is mostly composed of various seeds and grains. They will, however, also consume a wide variety of small creatures, ranging from insects to vertebrates such as frogs and lizards. Their chicks are able to feed themselves within a day of hatching. Platte River, Kearney, Nebraska.

FAR RIGHT: Sandhill Cranes (*Grus canadensis*) have well-developed legs—their chicks are able to run within a day of hatching—and because of this are referred to as "colts." Socorro, Bosque del Apache, New Mexico, USA.

RIGHT: Unlike other members of the heron family, Great Egrets (*Casmerodius albus*) do not feed at night. They do, however, search for similar prey, either individually or in small mixed groups. Avery Island, Louisiana, USA.

BELOW: There are a number of species of egret seen in North America. The Great Egret is the most common. It is seen from Florida all the way into Southern Canada during the warmer months and its range is shown here.

Year Round

Summer (breeding)

Winter (non-breeding)

Migration

LEFT: Like other herons, the Little Blue Heron is an adept hunter and will eat almost any small animal it can catch. Its diet is primarily composed of fish, amphibians, and aquatic invertebrates. During the breeding season it is distributed across the southeastern United States; however, it also occurs throughout Central America and the northern parts of South America. Fort De Soto County Park, Florida, USA.

LEFT: Great Blue Herons are distributed throughout Central and North America during the spring and summer. Some then migrate south as far as South America during the winter. They live near water and can be found in or alongside lakes, marshes, rivers, swamps, and shorelines, where they hunt for small animals. Manasota, Florida, USA.

BELOW: There are six common species of herons in North America, of which the Great Blue Heron is the most abundant. Its range is shown here as an example.

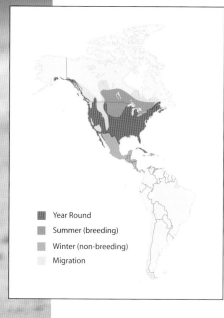

■ Year Round
■ Summer (breeding)
■ Winter (non-breeding)
■ Migration

RIGHT: The Great Blue Heron has legs that are much longer than those of other members of the heron family. Consequently, it is able to wade through much deeper water in search of its prey. Florida, USA.

FAR RIGHT: The Sandhill Crane is a tall, migratory wading bird that spends the winter in parts of the southern United States and northern Mexico. With the coming of spring, it flies north to breed, with some populations choosing to nest as far north as northern Alaska. Platte River, Nebraska, USA.

LEFT: The Sandhill Crane—this one is little more than a nestling—breeds in wetlands such as marshes and bogs, where they build their nests on floating vegetation. When the chicks hatch, they are covered with fine, browned-colored down and are able to walk within a very short time.

RIGHT: The Green Heron is unusual in the bird world in that it often throws bait onto the water's surface to lure small fish with reach of its powerful beak. This bait may take the form of anything from insects to feathers. Florida, USA.

RIGHT: Although the Great Blue Heron (*Ardea herodias*) has a very thin neck, it is able to control its muscles in such a way that it is able to swallow fish that are several times wider. Florida Keys, USA.

FAR RIGHT: The White Ibis is a wading bird that is found only in hot regions, including the southernmost parts of the U.S., as well as Central and northern South America. It uses its long, curved beak to probe for small creatures in soft mud and soil. Florida, USA.

BELOW: The range of the White Ibis.

Year Round

Summer (breeding)

Winter (non-breeding)

Migration

LEFT: The Reddish Egret's range is confined to the hotter parts of the North American continent, including Florida, Texas, and Mexico. It is also found in the Caribbean and along the north coast of South America. It hunts for fish and other small creatures in shallow salt water. Fort DeSoto Park, Florida, USA.

RIGHT: The Snowy Egret has a massive range—it is distributed from the northernmost regions of the U.S. to southern South America—and it can be found in a variety of wetland areas. It is easily distinguished from similar birds by its black legs and yellow feet. St. Augustine, Florida, USA.

RIGHT: The Tricolored Heron (formerly known as the Louisiana Heron) is found across much of the southeastern United States. It is a medium sized bird that, as can be seen here, is an accomplished hunter. It will capture and consume anything from fish to frogs, as the opportunity arises. Fort DeSoto Park, Florida, USA.

FAR RIGHT: Silhouettes of two Sandhill Cranes. Bosque del Apache National Wildlife Refuge, New Mexico, USA.

Year Round

Summer (breeding)

Winter (non-breeding)

Migration

LEFT: The Roseate Spoonbill is a remarkable-looking bird that is found in the southernmost parts of the U.S., as well as Central America and northern South America. It has a very strange spoon-shaped bill that it uses to sift small plants and creatures from shallow water. Lee County, Florida, USA.

LEFT INSET: The range of the Roseate Spoonbill.

RIGHT: The Black-crowned Night-Heron has a greater range than any other heron in the world. It differs from other species in that it feeds at twilight and during the night. It will take a wide variety of prey and other foodstuffs, including snakes, mice, eggs, frogs, and fish. Louisiana, USA.

BELOW: The range of the Black-crowned Night-Heron.

Year Round
Summer (breeding)
Winter (non-breeding)
Migration

RIGHT: The Green Heron is a small wading bird that can be found across much of North America, more or less wherever there is sufficient water for it to find its prey. During the spring and summer it moves north to breed, but returns to more southerly regions during the winter. Osceola County, Florida, USA.

FAR RIGHT: A Reddish Egret—in the white phase—dancing on a blue strip of Estero Lagoon. Fort Myers Beach, Florida, USA.

Woodpeckers, Sapsuckers, and Flickers

The woodpeckers, sapsuckers, and flickers all belong to the same family, the Picidae. There are twenty-three species that regularly live and breed in North America, if you include the rare (and possibly extinct) Ivory-billed Woodpecker. They are all birds that have special adaptations to help them find food inside the trunks of trees. Typically, woodpeckers hunt for the larvae of various wood-boring insects, such as beetles and moths. In order to reach them, the birds have pointed, chisel-like beaks with which they hammer away at the wood—this creates the well-known woodpecker "drumming" sound. The high-impact loads delivered by this rapid hammer-pecking would stun most living things very quickly. These fascinating birds, however, have specially thickened skulls as well as various other adaptations to prevent pecking-induced injuries. Once the bird has successfully located an insect grub and made an access hole, it inserts a long, thin tongue that has a barb-like structure on the end that grips the hapless insect—it is then dragged out for consumption. Woodpeckers also use their beaks to make a drumming sound that they use both as a territorial signaling system, and as a method of locating any insect larvae within the wood they are searching.

Other members of the family hunt in different ways—the Wryneck, for instance, is a small bird that visits North America occasionally when it crosses over into Alaska from Eurasia. It hunts for food on the ground, and is especially adept at catching ants using what is said to be the longest tongue of any bird. Another bird in this group that spends much of its feeding time on the ground is the Northern Flicker. Like the Wryneck, it eats ants; however, it will also take other insects—often on the wing—as well as fruits, berries, seeds, and nuts. There are two variants of this species—the Yellow-shafted Flicker, which is found in eastern North America, and the Red-shafted Flicker, which resides in western North America.

Sapsuckers are very similar to woodpeckers in that they also use their beaks to make holes in trees. They do not hunt for insects within the wood, but instead drink the sap that bleeds from the holes they have made. Insects that are attracted to the leaking sap are eaten, however. Sapsuckers choose different tree and shrub species depending on the time of year, with birch being especially favored during the breeding season. There are only four species of sapsuckers, and all of them are found in North America.

Although most of the birds in this family are often quite noisy, they are generally shy and are rarely seen. Some species, such as the Downy Woodpecker, however, will visit gardens if food is put out for them. They favor fat-based food, such as oil-rich seeds, suet, and peanut butter. Most of the woodpeckers also use their sharp beaks to make nest holes in suitable trees. Typically, the nest chamber is situated between 6 and 18 inches below the hole and is lined with woodchips.

FAR LEFT: The Red-headed Woodpecker is found in southern parts of Canada, and across much of the central United States. During the winter it moves to the south of this range, returning north again in the spring. It favors woodlands, forests, and orchards, as well as agricultural areas, although it will also visit gardens. Rondeau Provincial Park, Ontario, Canada.

LEFT: The Hairy Woodpecker is a black-and-white striped bird that, like all in the woodpecker family, has a chisel-like beak. It prefers to live in recently burned forest areas. This trait, however, has led to a decline in its population where fires are not allowed to burn naturally. McLeansville, North America, USA.

BELOW: The range of the Hairy Woodpecker is shown as an example of the spread of woodpeckers in North America, it being the most widespread species.

Year Round
Summer (breeding)
Winter (non-breeding)
Migration

RIGHT: The Golden-fronted Woodpecker is distributed through Texas and Oklahoma and down into the tropics. It feeds on various kinds of fruit, especially those found on cacti. The male has a red cap, whereas the female's is black. Both sexes have a golden patch above the beak. Edinburg, Texas, USA.

RIGHT: The Yellow-bellied Sapsucker is a migratory woodpecker that is well known for making a distinctive drumming sound at the start of the breeding season. It breeds in southern Canada and the northern U.S. During the winter it inhabits warm areas from the southeastern United States to Panama. McLeansville, North Carolina, USA.

BELOW: The range of the Yellow-bellied Sapsucker.

Year Round
Summer (breeding)
Winter (non-breeding)
Migration

FAR RIGHT: The Northern Flicker feeds mainly on ants and other insects, however, they can be attracted to garden feeders if suet is put out for them on a regular basis. McLeansville, North Carolina, USA.

FAR RIGHT INSET: The range of the Northern Flicker.

Year Round

Summer (breeding)

Winter (non-breeding)

Migration

LEFT: The Pileated Woodpecker is about 15 inches high, making it the largest woodpecker in North America. It is a bird of coniferous and deciduous forests, where it feeds on various insects—especially carpenter ants and beetle larvae—as well as fruits and nuts. Florida, USA.

RIGHT: The Red-bellied Woodpecker is distributed across much of the eastern part of North America, where it is one of the most commonly seen woodpeckers. It eats a wide variety of foods, ranging from seeds and fruits to small animals. In harsh winters it migrates to southern climates, where it stays until spring.

LEFT: Although populations of Pileated Woodpeckers (*Dryocopus pileatus*) have been increasing in recent years, conservation measures are still vital to their survival. They are reliant on large pine trees with thick trunks, however, these are few and far between nowadays thanks to modern forestry practices. Moran State Park, Orcas Island.

LEFT: The Northern Flicker is a common bird that is often seen on the ground feeding on ants. Unlike woodpeckers, flickers do not have such heavily-built beaks, so they are unable to chisel into particularly hard tree trunks. They will, however, dig insects such as beetle grubs out of rotten logs and soft wood.

LEFT: The Red-bellied Woodpecker—like many others in the same family, stores nuts and seeds in cracks and holes in trees, fences and other convenient places.

FAR LEFT: The Gila Woodpecker lives in Sonoran Desert regions where it feeds on cactus fruit and various berries, as well as insects. It nests in holes it makes in the columns of saguaro and cardon cacti. It abandons the holes at the end of the breeding season, whereupon they are often taken over by other birds.

LEFT: Pileated Woodpeckers were denoted as endangered species for many years, however, their numbers have since recovered and they have been removed from the list. Pennsylvania, USA

RIGHT: The Yellow-shafted Flicker is an eastern race of the Northern Flicker. Recent surveys suggest that its populations are declining throughout its range, although the reasons for this are not yet fully understood. It is possible that the use of garden pesticides may be partly responsible. USA

Reference

Websites

The A.O.U. Check-list of North American Birds, Seventh Edition
http://www.aou.org/checklist/index.php3

The American Birding Association
http://www.americanbirding.org/index.html
http://www.americanbirding.org/checklist/index.html

American Eagle Foundation
http://www.eagles.org/
http://www.eagles.org/otherbirds.html

Birds of the Continental United States and Canada (part of Baltimore County Public Library)
http://www.bcpl.net/~tross/nabirds.html

Baltimore Bird Club (a chapter of the Maryland Ornithological Society)
http://baltimorebirdclub.org/

Birding and ecological sites in CASCADIA—MASSES OF LINKS (more than 1000)!
http://www.scn.org/earth/tweeters/links.html
http://www.scn.org/earth/tweeters/links.html#nor

American Bird Conservatory
http://www.abcbirds.org/

Hummingbirds.net
http://www.hummingbirds.net/bibliography.html

Bibliography

American Ornithologists Union; *The AOU Checklist of North American Birds*, 7th ed; Allen Press, Lawrence, Kansas, 1998.

Baughman, Mel; *National Geographic Reference Atlas to the Birds of North America*; National Geographic Society, Washington, DC, 2003.

Bull, J. and J. Farrand, Jr.; *National Audubon Society Field Guide to North American Birds: Eastern Region*; Alfred A. Knopf, New York, 1998.

LEFT: A flock of flamingos surely ranks as one of the greatest spectacles to be seen in nature.

Clark, William S. and Wheeler, Brian K. Hawks; *Peterson Field Guide Series* (Roger Tory Peterson, Ed.); Houghton Miflin, Boston, 1987.

Eastman, J.; *Birds of Forest, Yard, & Thicket*; Stackpole Books, Mechanicsburg, PA, 1997.

Eastman, J.; *Birds of Lake, Pond and Marsh*; Stackpole Books, Mechanicsburg, PA, 1999.

Eastman, J.; *Birds of Field and Shore*; Stackpole Books, Mechanicsburg, PA, 2000.

Ehrlich, P.R., D.S. Dobkin and D. Wheye; *The Birder's Handbook*; Simon & Schuster/Fireside, New York, 1988.

Farrand Jr., J. (Ed.); T*he Audubon Society Master Guide to Birding, Vols. 1 – 3*; Alfred A. Knopf, New York, 1983.

Greenewalt, Crawford H.; *Hummingbirds*; Dover Publications, 1990.

Griggs, J.; *American Bird Conservancy's Field Guide to All the Birds of North America*; Harper Collins, New York, 1997.

Hehner, M., C. Dorsey and G. Breining; *North American Game Birds*; Cy DeCosse Inc. Minnetonka, MN. 1996.

Johnsgard, P.A.; *Hawks, Eagles, and Falcons of North America*; Smithsonian Institute Press, Washington, DC, 1990.

Kaufman, K.; *Birds of North America*; Houghton Mifflin Co. Boston. 2000.

National Geographic; *National Geographic Field Guide to the Birds of North America, 3rd Ed*; National Geographic Society, Washington, DC, 1999.

Peterson, R. T.; *A Field Guide to Western Birds, 3rd Ed*; Houghton Mifflin Co., Boston, 1990.

Sibley, David Allen; *The Sibley Guide to Birds*; Alfred A. Knopf, New York, 2000.

Sibley, David Allen; *The Sibley Guide to Bird Life & Behavior*; Alfred A. Knopf, New York, 2001.

Sibley, David Allen; *Sibley's Birding Basics*; Alfred A. Knopf, New York, 2002.

Sibley, David Allen; *The Sibley Field Guide to Birds of Eastern North*

America; Alfred A. Knopf, New York, 2003.

Sibley, David Allen; *The Sibley Field Guide to Birds of Western North America*; Alfred A. Knopf, New York, 2003.

True, Dan; *Hummingbirds of North America: Attracting, Feeding, and Photographing*; University of New Mexico Press, 1993.

Wheeler, B.K. and W.S. Clark; *A Photographic Guide to North American Raptors*; Academic Press, New York, USA,, 1995.

Journals

Journal of Raptor Research—Produced by the Raptor Research Foundation, a professional society concerned with the study and conservation of birds of prey. Their website: http://biology.boisestate.edu/raptor/

International Zoo Yearbook—The International Zoo Yearbook is published by The Zoological Society of London as a service to zoos around the world. It acts as a forum for the exchange of information on the role of zoos in the conservation of biodiversity, specie, and habitats. The Zoological Society of London, Dept IZY, Regent's Park, London NWI 4RY UK. Tel: 020 7449 6281. Fax: 020 7449 6411. Email: yearbook@zsl.org

Organizations

National Audubon Society, 700 Broadway, New York, NY, 10003-9562. www.audubon.org

New York State Department of Environmental Conservation, 50 Wolf Road, Albany, NY 12233

New York State Wildlife Rehabilitation Council, Box 551, Tully, NY 13159

North American Raptor Breeders' Association. 540 N. 3rd St., Philadelphia, PA 19123

The Peregrine Fund, Inc., World Center for Birds of Prey, 5666W. Flying Hawk Lane, Boise, ID 83709

United States Fish and Wildlife Service, P.O. Box 779, Hadley, MA 01035

LEFT: Flamingos have mastered the art of balancing on one leg for long periods as they rest.

ABOVE: Songbirds enrich our environment in many ways—their beautiful early morning choruses help us start the day, while their wonderful plumage adds colour to our gardens and parks.

PAGE 256: Marshlands provide a rich habitat for a wide variety of bird species.